Afreeism

AFREEISM

How a New (and Ancient) Understanding
of the Universe Can Transform
Society and Enrich Our Lives

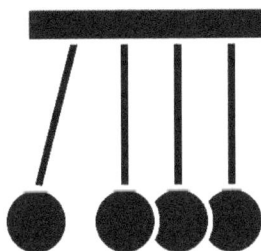

Stephen G. Marks

Two Eggs and Toast Press

Other Books by Stephen Marks:

Managerial Economics (with W. Samuelson and J Zagorsky)
Eighth Edition, Wiley, 2021

Becoming a Bilingual Family (with Jeffrey Marks)
University of Texas Press, 2013

For information contact:
The Afreeist Society
171 School Street
Boston, MA 02119
http://www.afreeism.org

Book and Cover design by Jeffrey Marks
ISBN: 978-1-7369874-0-7

First Edition: June 2021

DEDICATION

To Mary, Olivia, Claire, and Saraí
To my brother Jim
To David

CONTENTS

ACKNOWLEDGMENTS

First and foremost, I thank my brother Jeff without whom this project would never have happened. He was instrumental in all aspects of the book including proofreading (both technical and analytical), formatting, cover design, and production, as well as being the sounding board for the ideas in this book. He took the project on as if it were his own, and I so appreciate that. I thank my wife Mary for giving me the time, space, and sustenance (physical, mental, and emotional) to write and for her willingness to participate in the many discussions about the ideas in the book. I thank David Akiba for our many talks. I thank all those who have read drafts and who have given me input, including, but not limited to, my brother Dennis, my late brother Jim, my daughters Olivia and Claire, Alex Burke, William Burke, Etienne Deffarges, Diana Ensor, Elaine Hackney, Jock Harkness, Lisa Hiserodt, Mary Beth Holman, Tom Jacobson, John Maxfield, Robert Maxfield, and Paulette Tomasson. I thank my research assistants Mallory Madeiros, Jesse Lopes, Marcos Cabello, Alexander Bernstein, and Aaron Gordon. I thank Boston University, and especially the School of Law, which has given me the kind of job that allows me to write about anything that captures my fancy. I thank my friends who, although they may have not been directly involved in the production of this book, nevertheless gave me the support I needed to write and maintain some semblance of sanity during this terrible pandemic. Finally, I thank Lorraine, whose house I camped out at for months during some very difficult times for us both.

Introduction

IN THIS BOOK I PRESENT one fundamental idea. Yet it is an idea so powerful that, if fully embraced, it radically alters the way we see the world. It changes how we view each other and how we treat one another. It shakes up our conceptions of the good society and of good social policy. It makes us better people, removes impediments to our happiness, and increases the joy we find in life.

It is an idea based in science and reason, requiring no leaps of faith. It is an idea whose origins date back over two millennia, and at the same time is rooted in modern scientific discovery. It is not an easy idea. It requires abandoning a worldview that we probably have never questioned, a worldview that we take for granted, a worldview that affects our actions daily.

What is this radical yet ancient idea? It is simply this: we have no free will. The universe is a web of causation dating back to the beginning of time. Our actions are a part of this web. Although we feel that we are making decisions through free will, this is just an illusion. We could not have acted differently than we did.

Consider the case of Charles Whitman. Accounts describe the ex-Marine as intelligent, attractive, and a family man. In August 1966, after killing his mother and wife, Whitman climbed the tower at the University of Texas and

1

began shooting with a hunting rifle. In all, he killed 13 people and injured over 30. Neuroscientist Robert Sapolsky describes the scene:

> Whitman was literally an Eagle Scout and a childhood choirboy, a happily married engineering major with an IQ in the 99th percentile. In the prior year he had seen doctors, complaining of severe headaches and violent impulses (e.g., to shoot people from the campus tower). He left notes by the bodies of his wife and his mother, proclaiming love and puzzlement at his actions: "I cannot rationaly [sic] pinpoint any specific reason for killing her," and "let there be no doubt in your mind that I loved this woman with all my heart." His suicide note requested an autopsy of his brain, and that any money he had be given to a mental health foundation. The autopsy proved his intuition correct—Whitman had a glioblastoma tumor pressing on his amygdala.[1]

The amygdala is the part of the brain most responsible for aggression. Experts disagree on the role of the malignant tumor in influencing Whitman's actions. Other factors in Whitman's life could have influenced his behavior or interacted with the tumor. Whitman, because he died at the scene, never had to face a criminal judgment.

This story, and thought experiments derived from it, challenge our conceptions of moral responsibility and free will. Let us suppose that the police captured Whitman, rather than killing him. Let us further suppose that it was definitively proven that Whitman's tumor caused his actions. Finally, let us suppose that Whitman subsequently underwent surgery to remove the malignancy and that after the surgery psychological testing determined that Whitman had no violent or antisocial impulses at all. That is, he was returned to his former state in which he was a loving husband and son and a responsible member of the community. Would we feel justified in punishing him for his crime?

The fundamental thesis of this book is that we all are, in a sense, like Charles Whitman. That is, causal factors determine all of our actions. None of us possess free will. This is not a new notion. Indeed, some philosophers came to this conclusion several millennia ago and it represents the views of many philosophers and scientists today. In the next few chapters, I will present the arguments, both old and new, to support this view, as well as dive into the ancient origins of this idea.

The primary project of this book, however, is what to do with the knowledge that there is no free will. By synthesizing insights from various past and present religious and philosophical schools, I hope I can contribute to resolving that question. The implications of rejecting the idea of free will can be troubling. However, I hope to show that acceptance of this idea can result both in a better society and in a more joyful life. The Stoics, the Buddhists, the Confucianists, and a number of prominent philosophers understood this. Without free will, there can be no moral responsibility for past actions. Without moral responsibility, there can be no regret, remorse, guilt, or shame. There can be no retribution. The criminal justice system will continue to function, but in an altered, more humane way. We will treat each other with more tolerance and compassion; we will treat *ourselves* with more tolerance and compassion. Life will become more joyful. These are all big claims, but they are amply supported in the following chapters.

I will use the word *freeism* (free'-ism) for the belief in free will and moral responsibility and *freeist* for someone who adheres to these beliefs. I will define an *afreeist* (ay'-free-ist) as someone who does not have a belief in free will or moral responsibility. I realize that these are not the most elegant terms. Except for the English root, I am following the convention of theist and atheist. A theist believes in a god or gods. An atheist does not have this belief. Thus, atheism and afreeism are both defined as an absence of belief.

There is no scientific evidence indicating the existence of free will. To the contrary, there is much scientific evidence against it. This evidence comes from the idea of causation. The idea of causation is that outcomes are determined by inputs. On a pool table, if a cue ball of a particular size, weight, and plasticity collides with another ball of a particular size, weight, and plasticity and does so at a particular angle and speed, the latter ball will move at a determined angle and speed. Depending on the angle, the speed of the ball, the resistance of the felt on the table, etc., the struck ball may eventually fall into a pocket. If we know enough about the inputs, we can predict the output.

Almost all of us accept the idea of causation and use it for most aspects of our lives. We put toast in the toaster because we know that, if we push the lever down, an electrical circuit will be completed, which will provide electricity to the heating elements, which will heat the bread causing a chemical reaction (which chemists call oxidation), resulting in a warm brown piece of toast, which we can then butter (we know that the heat will cause the butter to melt) and perhaps even put a bit a jam on. This will cause a pleasant sensation in our mouths as we chew and swallow our creation.

The idea of causation has allowed us to do some pretty remarkable things, and also some pretty awful things. The laws of physics embody the idea of causation. Scientists employ these laws to create rockets and spacecraft and to put people on the moon. Using causation, scientists and engineers have created smartphones and laptop computers. Biologists have been able to cure or vaccinate against terrible diseases, such as smallpox, polio, and many strains of influenza. Unfortunately, we have also exploited our knowledge of causation to create weapons of mass destruction and to wage horrible wars.

It seems clear that almost everybody assumes that causation applies to most events. Many scientists and philosophers, finding causation wherever they look, have concluded that causation is universal. That is, all events have causes. Indeed, if we knew all of the causes preceding an event, we could accurately predict what will occur. This applies to toasting toast in a toaster, but also to seemingly random events like flipping a coin. If we knew everything about the inputs, we could predict which side the coin would land on. (Some scientists and philosophers make an exception for quantum mechanics, which operates at the subatomic level. More on this later.)

The idea that inputs determine all outcomes is known as determinism. Determinism is a theory, much like evolution, or the theory of gravity. Like these theories, there is strong evidence to support it and no evidence that contradicts it.

Nevertheless, the idea that *all* outcomes are caused is not universally accepted. I believe that it is safe to say that most people, including some philosophers and scientists, believe that humans possess free will—that is, that humans possess the ability to make a choice among various alternatives, a choice that is not dictated by strictly causal factors. The notion that we have free will figures in the judgments we make about people and, at times, in the consequences that we impose when people make the wrong choice. We consider people to be good and worthy of admiration if they make good moral choices. Likewise, we condemn people who make bad moral choices and sometimes ridicule people for making silly, irrational, or ill-considered choices. We may punish people for making socially detrimental choices. (For example, we may impose a jail sentence on someone who chooses to rob a bank.)

The notion that humans possess free will and that with it comes moral responsibility is so ingrained that few people probably ever think about it. Nevertheless, more than two millennia ago, some philosophers and scientists concluded that the universe is completely deterministic. Most prominent among them were Leucippus and Democritus (proponents of the atomic theory of matter) and the Stoics. More recently, Baruch Spinoza, writing in the 1600s, concluded that such determinism precluded free will. Schopenhauer and Nietzsche also rejected free will. In modern times, these doubters of free will include prominent social and physical scientists, including the late physicist Stephen Hawking, evolutionary biologist Jerry Coyne, neuroscientist Robert Sapolsky, cognitive scientists Wolf Singer and Paul Bloom, and philosopher Derk Pereboom, just to name a few. Their argument is simple. If everything is caused, then the world has to unfold along a determined path. Choices that appear to be free are not. A person may have done what he or she desired, but the desires were caused by previous inputs. These inputs, in turn, were caused by other inputs. We can go further and further back through the chain of causation. The result is that the choice that a person makes is caused by inputs that existed even before that person was born. Thus, universal causation negates the possibility of free will. The world and the choices people make unfold in only one way.

In this book, I would like to persuade you that those philosophers and scientists who reject free will, having found no evidence of it, are correct. In doing so, I will lean heavily on arguments that they have presented throughout history. (The arguments have not changed much since the days of Spinoza.)

If free will is an illusion, then it is an illusion held by many, many people. The question is why? It can be argued that the concept of free will, like the concept of a god, is a social evolutionary adaptation. That is, some beliefs may contribute to society even if they are not true. A society whose members believe in free will may be more likely to survive than a society whose members do not believe in free will.

In his highly entertaining, provocative, and insightful book, *Sapiens*, Yuval Noah Harari, makes two major points regarding this evolutionary adaptation. The first is that the capacity to develop and hold beliefs in fictional entities (such as the belief in a god, in a nation, or in a corporation) is an evolutionary advantage for the species *homo sapiens* which not only allowed the species to win out over other species of man (such as *homo neanderthalensis*) but also over other animals. In Harari's conception, myths allowed (and allow) *homo sapiens* to organize and coordinate in vast numbers. In contrast, without myths and depending only on bonds of kinship and friendship, animals (such as apes or other species of humans) could not organize in groups greater than 150 members or so. Myths allowed *homo sapiens* to organize in vast numbers and to overwhelm their less organized competition.

The belief in free will, and the corresponding belief in moral responsibility, may be one of those organizing myths. Societies whose members believe in free will may do better than those whose members do not so believe. The belief in free will leads to self-sanctions (guilt, remorse, regret) and social sanctions (fines, incarceration, shaming) against those who, out of their own free will, decide to engage in antisocial activity—activity that is harmful to the organization of society and thus to its survival.

(The irony of this may not be lost on some readers. Behavior modification is based on a causal model of behavior. That is, if we have the right inputs, in the form of the appropriate rewards or sanctions, then these will cause the right behavior. Yet we justify the application of rewards and sanctions through the notion of free will, which postulates that human behavior is not causally determined.)

Note that, in Harari's account, not all myths are useful to the survival of *homo sapiens*. Myths are like viruses. They spread throughout society with little regard for the benefit of the species or of individuals. Nevertheless, if a belief contributes to the downfall of the society, it will die along with its societal host. Only those beliefs that benefit society will survive. The belief in free will may be one of these evolutionarily favored beliefs.

If we believe that free will is a useful myth for society to organize and thrive, why not just accept the myth and move on? There are several reasons for exposing the truth. The first is that it is simply the nature of science and philosophy to seek the truth, wherever it may lead. In such a view, the philosopher and the scientist are committed to finding the truth and the consequences be damned. As such, it may be inevitable that this myth must fall. As Harari states:

> [A] huge gulf is opening between the tenets of liberal humanism and the latest findings of the life sciences, a gulf we cannot ignore much longer. Our liberal political and judicial systems are founded on the belief that every individual has a sacred inner nature, indivisible and immutable, which gives meaning to the world, and which is the source of all ethical and political authority. This is a reincarnation of the traditional Christian belief in a free and eternal soul that resides within each individual. Yet

over the last 200 years, the life sciences have thoroughly undermined this belief. Scientists studying the inner workings of the human organism have found no soul there. They increasingly argue that human behaviour is determined by hormones, genes and synapses, rather than by free will—the same forces that determine the behaviour of chimpanzees, wolves, and ants. Our judicial and political systems largely try to sweep such inconvenient discoveries under the carpet. But in all frankness, how long can we maintain the wall separating the department of biology from the departments of law and political science?[2]

If this convenient myth does fall, what then of society? What happens to moral responsibility, for example? This fear is not just a recent one. In response to Democritus's view of determinism, Epicurus, in his *Letter to Menoeceus*, wrote:

> It is better to follow the myth about the gods than to be a
> slave of the "fate" of the physicists: for the former suggests
> a hope of forgiveness, in return for honor, but the latter
> has an ineluctable necessity.[3]

It is of some comfort that we have been here before. The concern that a loss of faith in free will could have serious societal impacts mirrors concern over the loss of faith in the existence of a god. If there is no belief in a god, what anchors the moral fabric of society? What stops people from lying, cheating, stealing, or even murdering, when it is to their advantage to do so?

I believe that these concerns are unjustified. In the case of religion, a majority of the populations in many European countries have given up on a belief in a god. Yet, European societies continue to function. Indeed, one can argue that Europeans do much better than Americans in terms of social activity. For example, crime rates, including rates of violent crime, in continental Europe are significantly lower than those in the United States, where there is a high degree of religiosity. This is not because Europeans have given up myths altogether. Harari suggests that liberal humanism, another myth, provides much of what religion did previously. However, losing faith in a god did not entail the loss of civilization as we know it. I believe that society will survive a loss of faith in free will as well.

And, of course, a loss of faith in free will is not inevitable. Americans, or at least a large majority of them, may never lose faith in free will. The United States has seemed relatively resistant to erosions of faith in a god, in spite of the success of science and philosophy in providing descriptions of the world and the place of humans in it. Likewise, despite what philosophers and scientists claim, American society will likely resist a loss of faith in free will. The idea of free will is so strongly held that it seems unlikely that a majority of the population would reject it, no matter how strong the philosophical arguments or the scientific evidence.

But what if we could shake the belief in free will and moral responsibility? I believe that if the general population stopped believing in free will, both society and the individuals in it would be better off. Previously, I stated that Harari's book Sapiens had two important theses. One, described above, is that myths have enabled (and continue to enable) humans to coordinate activity in great numbers, thereby overwhelming other species. The second great thesis of Harari's book, however, is that belief systems that may make the species more successful (the belief in a god, nationalism, liberal humanism, free will), do not necessarily make the *individuals* in those societies happier or better off.

Introduction

Therefore, while society may thrive, individuals bear the brunt of the myth.

I believe that humans, as a species, no longer need the myth of free will to survive and thrive. Furthermore, the belief in free will, while perhaps helping humans to proliferate and dominate in the past, makes individuals unhappy.

In this book, I will try to convince you that, by jettisoning our faith in free will, we not only will see the world the way it truly is, we will also make the world and our lives better.

We will support social policies that are both more humane and more effective. This applies particularly in the area of criminal justice, but also to many other areas of government policy.

We will act more generously towards other people in our personal lives. Our behavior towards each other will improve. In particular, we will become more tolerant and more accepting of other people, their life situations, and their actions.

We will improve our attitude towards ourselves by mitigating feelings of guilt, regret, remorse, and self-blame, all of which are impediments to a joyful life.

In all, accepting the world the way it is, accepting that there is no free will, completely changes how we view ourselves and other people. It affects what we believe is good in the world. The change is profound. I argue that it is profoundly good. If taken seriously, this idea changes the world for the better.

This book has two goals. One is to convince you that free will does not exist. I undertake this in Part I. In this part, I marshal facts and logic to argue that a belief in free will is not justified. The second goal is to explore the implications of this, to glean lessons for living from this understanding.

This is a more difficult task than the first and I devote Parts II and III to it. We will enlist the services of the Stoics of ancient Greece and Rome, of the Buddha and Confucius, of the philosophers of the Enlightenment, and of present-day thinkers and scientists. With their help, we will examine what afreeism says about how we can best live our lives. I will argue that, if we take afreeism to heart, we can improve the world and our own lives.

One caveat before we start: it is always important to be humble about what we can know about the workings of the universe. We shall see that current evidence overwhelmingly supports the model of causation and the consequent absence of free will. Nevertheless, new evidence may always emerge and lead to new understandings. As scientists and philosophers, we must always approach this and any other subject with an open mind and be willing to change. With that caveat, I present to you both the arguments for afreeism and a tentative guide for living.

Part I

The Basics of Afreeism

Chapter 1

The Illusion of Free Will

MOST PEOPLE COME TO DISCUSSIONS about free will believing—and wanting—it to exist. Life without free will does not make sense to many people, so questioning its existence is often a hard sell. Free will is comforting. It means that you have some control over your life. It means that you are responsible for your actions. It means that you can hold yourself and others accountable.

The idea of free will forms the basis of our system of social control. If someone commits an act that society has deemed illegal, we punish the perpetrator. But we do so only if the person who committed the act did so of her own free will. Someone who speeds down the freeway is likely to receive a ticket. However, if the driver is the victim of a carjacking and is speeding because someone in the passenger seat is holding a gun to her head, then we excuse her behavior. It was not an act of free will.

Yet this is an illusion. At a fundamental level, causal forces acted on both drivers. The firing of nerve cells (neurons) in the brain caused both actions. These firings were caused by other firings, which were stimulated by others, and so on. Some of these firings were triggered by stimulations from the environment. If we could trace the path of causation, we would see that it goes back in time indefinitely, back before these two drivers were even born. Thus, in both cases, speeding was the only outcome possible. Where then is the free will?

Below I will present arguments as to why free will is an illusion. Please keep in mind, however, that the burden of proof regarding the existence of free will is with those who assert its existence. Indeed, the burden of proof regarding the existence of anything is with those who assert the existence of that thing. If you are arguing that there is such a thing as unicorns, then the burden is on you to show that they exist. This also applies to other things such as to the existence of bears (of which there is plenty of evidence), of a god, or of free will. It will probably come as no shock to the reader that I believe that bears exist, but that I have seen scant scientific evidence of the existence of unicorns or free will. In spite of this burden of proof, free will is such a powerful illusion that I do feel compelled to at least sketch out the arguments against its existence. So here they are.

A Definition of Free Will

Before we analyze the evidence, we must know what we are talking about. What exactly is free will? I would like to start by defining free will the way a person on the street (or the writer of a dictionary trying to capture the popular meaning) might define it. The Merriam Webster's Dictionary defines free will as follows:

The Illusion of Free Will

free will, noun

1: voluntary choice or decision

   Example: I do this of my own free will.

2: freedom of humans to make choices that are not determined by prior causes or by divine intervention

The first definition tells us nothing. In common parlance, the word *voluntary* is simply a synonym of *of one's free will*. It is identical to say that I do something voluntarily and to say that I do something of my own free will. Thus, the first definition does not help us.

The second definition is more edifying. It asserts that some actions are determined by prior causes (or by a god) while others are choices that are *not* determined by prior causes or by a divine being. Of course, even with this definition, the freedom implied by free will is never unlimited. I cannot choose to flap my arms and fly. Likewise, a driver who comes to an intersection may be able to go right or left, but the path straight ahead may be blocked by a police officer or a barricade. The definition implies, however, that when presented with alternatives, a person may choose among them and that that choice among the alternatives is not determined by prior causes or by divine intervention. This is sometimes called the freedom to do otherwise. Free will thus depends on the freedom to do otherwise.

(Some philosophers define free will quite unconventionally so as not to depend on the freedom to do otherwise. I discuss these views in Chapter 4.)

The Evidence of Free Will

Now, what is the evidence that we humans possess free will? The primary piece of evidence is that in our daily experience it seems that we do have the ability to choose. In certain circumstances, we deliberate quite extensively, even agonizing over what choice to make. It seems as though we can choose among a number of alternatives. When we finally decide what we want, we choose one of those alternatives.

A second piece of evidence is that we observe instances in which people in similar positions make different choices. Perhaps we can explain these cases by free will.

A third consideration is that we believe in moral responsibility. That is, we believe that some of the choices we make are right and others are wrong. Someone who makes a wrong choice is responsible for that choice and we are justified in imposing negative consequences on that person. If someone chooses to rob a bank, cheat on her taxes, or violently assault another person, then we feel as if that robber, cheater, or assailant is responsible for her actions, and we feel justified in punishing her. But we only hold a person responsible and justify punishing her if she acted with free will. If someone caused her to take the action by, for example, holding a gun to her head, then we feel that she is not morally responsible, and therefore not worthy of punishment. It is hard to justify punishing someone if they lack free will. Because free will is seemingly a precondition to moral responsibility, and because humans tend to believe in moral responsibility, people tend to conclude that free will must exist.

For some, there may be theological justifications for free will to exist. Some may believe that free will exists simply because their canonical text (the Bible, the Quran, the Book of Mormon) says or implies that it does. Other more sophisticated theological arguments may exist as well. For example, if a religion posits a god that is both omnipotent and good, then we must account for a source of evil other than the god. So, how can we account for evil and injustice in the world? The answer is free will. The god grants free will to humans. Evil comes from the free choices of humans. It is humans who choose evil, not the god.

In my discussion below and in future chapters, I will return to and discuss more fully these arguments for free will. I will argue that the intuition that we have free will is an illusion. It may seem as if we could do otherwise, but we cannot. I will also argue that, because we do not have free will, we do not have moral responsibility for actions we have taken. (Before you run away, let me say that I will also argue that in some cases we can justify punishing someone even though the choice she made was determined by causes that began long before she was born. See Chapter 10.)

Causation

The debate over the existence of free will is inextricably linked to the notions of causation and determinism. The nature of causation is a philosophical question with a very long history, dating back at least to Leucippus and Democritus in fifth-century BCE Greece, if not earlier. (I discuss the history of thought on free will in Chapter 7.) For now, let us begin with a definition. A commonsense definition of causation is this:

A causes B (where A and B are states of the world) if and only if A and B both occur and:

1. A implies B, that is, if whenever state A occurs, then B also occurs, and

2. B occurs after A occurs.

This definition is not perfect. However, for our purposes, it will do.

Determinism

As we look at the physical world, particularly the nonhuman world, we generally see two types of events:

1. Events that are caused ("caused events")

2. Events that are random ("random events")

Consider caused events. A cue ball strikes another ball on a pool table at a certain angle and with a certain rotation. The movement of the second ball—and whether it ultimately drops into a pocket—depends on factors that were present before the second ball was struck by the first. These factors include the location, the velocity and direction of the cue ball, the amount of spin it has, its mass, the friction of the felt on the table, gravity, the mass and location of the second ball, the location of the pockets, and a host of other factors. If we knew all of these things, we could predict the path of the second ball and whether it would ultimately fall into the pocket.

Because events are caused, we can sometimes predict them, especially if the systems are simple enough. Often, however, systems are too complex to make accurate predictions. Still, we believe that such events are caused. Most people, even believers in free will, subscribe to the theory that most events are caused, and if we understand the causal chain, then we can predict them. Causation forms the basis of science and engineering. It has allowed us to construct cities, build computers and cellphones, and cure diseases.

Determinists hypothesize that *all* things have causes. The difference between a determinist and everyone else is that a determinist believes that everything has a cause, whereas everyone else believes only that *most* things are caused. Determinists believe that even supposed random events are caused. (That is, they are not truly random.) When we flip a coin, whether the coin lands heads up or tails up is completely determined by the force and angle of the flip, the physical characteristics of the coin itself (how hard or flexible it is, how much it weighs, what its exact shape is), the amount of air resistance and air currents, the physical properties of the surface on which it lands (its hardness, elasticity, etc.), and many other factors. Given the complexity of the action of flipping a coin, it is now impossible to predict whether the coin will land heads up or tails up. Thus, at least to us, the coin flip appears random. Determinists hypothesize that such events, even though they appear random, are caused; the laws of physics apply to all things. Indeed, even random number generators in computers are not truly random. (For those of you who are saying, "Hey, what about quantum mechanics?" we will get to that below.)

Determinists hypothesize that the best model of the universe is one that acknowledges that all things are caused (with the possible exception of quantum events.) Indeed, there is no evidence of an event ever happening that is uncaused or, at the quantum level, random. Determinists do not make exceptions for living organisms, no matter how complex. Actions by such organisms are determined by causal factors. Every action by an organism has been determined by causes that occur through complex interactions at the physical, chemical, and cellular levels, such as the way neurons interact with each other and with other cells. Like the coin flip, these complex interactions are hard to predict.

For example, when a dog's owner calls the dog, the dog must decide whether to come or not. At one level, the decision depends on the dog's training, the environment (is there a squirrel in sight?), and a host of other factors. On another level, whether the dog comes depends how the sound of the owner's voice triggers the nerve cells in the ear, and how this gets transmitted through other nerve cells to the brain, where yet more nerve cells interact in a very complex manner, and whether this ultimately sends electric impulses through additional nerve cells to muscle cells, resulting in the dog either coming to the owner or failing to. The interactions are incredibly complex, and while the result may not be easy to predict (especially if a squirrel is involved), the outcome is completely caused. What the dog does is determined. Given the set of inputs, it could not do otherwise.

The notion of causation is completely intuitive to many people and seems commonsense when applied to inanimate objects, such as billiard balls, and even to animals, such as dogs. Some people, however, find it hard to accept that such reasoning applies to humans and particularly to themselves. But there is no reason to suppose that it does not. As Sam Harris points out,

> The brain is a physical system, entirely beholden to the laws of nature—and there is every reason to believe that changes in its functional state and material structure entirely dictate our thoughts and actions.[4]

Consider a human action, such as kicking a football or expressing an opinion. As neuroscientist (and determinist)

Robert Sapolsky put it in an interview with National Public Radio Producer David Kestenbaum,

> A muscle did something. Meaning a neuron in your motor cortex commanded your muscle to do that. That neuron fired only because it got inputs from umpteen other neurons milliseconds before. And those neurons only fired because they got inputs milliseconds before and back and back and back. Show me one neuron anywhere in this pathway that, from out of nowhere, decided to say something that activated in ways that are not explained by the laws of the physical universe, and ions, and channels, and all that sort of stuff. Show me one neuron that has some cellular semblance of free will. And there is no such neuron.[5]

One Path

Determinism implies that everything unfolds one way. If determinism is true, everything has been determined since the dawn of time (currently hypothesized to be at the instant of the big bang), including all of our thoughts and actions, when and how we live, who we marry, what kids we have, where we live, how we conduct our lives, when we die, and even whether we will choose to have a cup of coffee this morning. When someone takes an action, it could not be otherwise. In other words, if we could unwind the universe back until the time of the big bang and let it run again with the same initial conditions, the universe would unfold in the exact same way.

There are huge implications to this. For purposes of our discussion, the most important implication is that we have no free will, at least as free will is conventionally defined. To be sure, we often do what we want because we want it, but what we want has been determined by a chain of causation. Therefore, the choice we make is likewise determined. In reality, we could do only one thing.

Neuroscience, Robotics, and Artificial Intelligence

In some ways, the progression of ideas on free will follows a similar—though not identical—path as that of evolution. A theory of evolution involving natural selection was proposed by Charles Darwin with the publication of the Origin of Species in 1859. The theory was so compelling and the evidence so convincing that it rapidly became the accepted theory among scientists, if not among the public. Later, additional scientific evidence, including genetics and the discovery of DNA, buttressed the theory.

Likewise, as far back as the time of ancient Greece, scientists and philosophers had convincing evidence that the universe is causal, and that free will is an illusion. As with evolution, additional discoveries have buttressed this idea. This new evidence comes from two major sources. On the one hand, advances in neuroscience have provided increasing amounts of evidence that decision-making in the brain is the result of causal interactions among neurons. Coming from a different direction, robotics and artificial intelligence have created more and more human-like machines. The decision-making of these machines has become less and less distinguishable from that of humans. Yet there is no claim that any of these machines are exercising free will.

The more one studies the brain, the more mechanical it appears. Thus, the major contribution of neuroscience to the issue of the existence of free will is that neuroscience confirms that the brain is subject to the same laws of physics, chemistry, and biology that the rest of the universe is subject to. That is why neuroscientists are among the biggest skeptics of the existence of free will. Here is neuroscientist Robert Sapolsky in the chapter of his book that discusses research findings on the effect of PFC (prefrontal cortex) neurons on behavior:

> A guy does something impulsive and awful and neuro-imaging reveals that, unexpectedly, he's missing all his PFC neurons. There's a dualist temptation now to view his behavior as more "biological" or "organic" in some nebulous manner than if he had committed the same act with a normal PFC. However, the guy's awful, impulsive act is equally "biological" with or without a PFC. The sole difference is that the workings of the PFC-less brain are easier to understand with our primitive research tools.[6]

In other words, all brain activity is causal. Sometimes we can trace the causal path, but often it is just too complex.

One does not have to be a neuroscientist to believe that the laws of physics apply to the brain as they do to every other piece of matter. Sapolsky laments that it took neuroscience to convince lawmakers in Congress that PTSD was real—that is, biological—because sufferers exhibited atrophy of the hippocampus when it was obvious clinically that PTSD was real, and that therefore it *had* to be biological. Indeed, all behavior *is* biological. All behavior is caused.

Robotics and artificial intelligence provide additional confirmatory evidence. Indeed, facets of the free will debate have entered the popular culture. The movie *Blade Runner* (based on Phillip Dick's novel, *Do Androids Dream of Electric Sheep?*) features "replicants," who are sophisticated human-like robots. In particular, several replicants have arrived on earth from the colonies and are searching for their maker in order to extend their lifespans. The replicants exhibit emotions and make decisions. One new-model replicant does not even realize that she is a replicant. (She has been given human memories.) Indeed, there is a debate about whether Harrison Ford's character, an investigator who tracks down and kills replicants, is himself a replicant. (The director says yes; the actor says no.[7]) This popular account challenges viewers to consider what is human. And, of course, who can forget Hal, the rogue computer in *2001, A Space Odyssey*. Human-like computers populate science fiction. One such computer, in Robert Heinlein's classic *The Moon Is a Harsh Mistress,* gains consciousness and makes decisions, seemingly on its own and for its own interests. (For the interested reader, I have included an appendix to this chapter that discusses the relevance of *conscious* decision-making to the free will debate.)

In the nonfiction world, advances in computer intelligence continue apace. The question as to whether machines can think has been around at least since Alan Turing's famous paper, "Computing Machinery and Intelligence,"[8] in 1950. In it, he proposed a test in which a human interrogator communicates (through a keypad and monitor) with both a human and a machine but does not know which is which. The interrogator asks questions. If the interrogator cannot distinguish which respondent is the machine, then we must conclude that the machine can think. To date, there is no convincing evidence of a machine passing the Turing test. Yet many AI experts predict that it will happen relatively soon.

Of course, passing the Turing test means making decisions that look like free will. (The machines must make choices.) Yet no one claims that these machines are anything but causal—that is, determined.

Findings in neuroscience and artificial intelligence are not necessary for the conclusion that the world is deterministic. Physics, chemistry, and biology all provide overwhelming evidence of a deterministic world. Even quantum mechanics indicates that the world is, if not causally deterministic, at least stochastically deterministic. (See below for a definition of stochastic determinism.) Rather, advances in neuroscience and artificial intelligence do for determinism what genetics and DNA did for evolution. They simply provide additional confirmatory evidence to the already overwhelming evidence that the world runs according to the laws of physics and that humans are not exempt from those laws. We live in a deterministic world.

Quantum Mechanics
and Chaos Theory

At this point, we must discuss one little wrinkle in the deterministic universe. As we discussed above, random events are generally determined events about which we do not have sufficient information to make predictions. The study of subatomic particles, however, has led to the theory of quantum mechanics, which includes the idea that there may be truly random events, at least at the subatomic level.

Quantum mechanical randomness can possibly affect the macro universe through chaotic interactions. Chaos theory holds that tiny effects can have large consequences. Here is a well-known description of a chaotic chain:

> For want of a nail, the shoe was lost;
> For want of the shoe, the horse was lost;
> For want of the horse, the rider was lost;

For want of the rider, the battle was lost;
For want of the battle, the kingdom was lost . . .[9]

Another well-known characterization of some chaotic systems is the "butterfly effect," a term popularized after meteorologist Edward Lorenz, at a conference presentation, posed the following question: "Does the flap of a butterfly's wing in Brazil set off a tornado in Texas?" The answer is that it could.

Chaotic phenomena are not necessarily—or even usually—random, even though they may be practically unpredictable.[10] When applied to quantum mechanics, however, chaos theory leaves open the possibility that subatomic interactions—which according to quantum mechanics may be truly random—could generate large effects thereby introducing true randomness into the universe. This has led some philosophers to believe that quantum randomness gives them an opening to argue for the existence of free will. Yet such an opening is illusory. Note the following:

1. It is still unclear whether there are truly random events. In other words, a deterministic model could someday displace quantum mechanical randomness. (Albert Einstein was famously skeptical of the randomness in quantum mechanics. "God does not play dice," he said.) Indeed, such models already exist, such as the De Broglie-Bohm theory, the many-worlds (multiverse) model pioneered by Hugh Everett III[11], and the more recent quantum causal model of Allen et al. (2017).

2. The quantum mechanical model is, at a minimum, stochastically deterministic. Even if there is true randomness, the probabilities are determined. That is, if two states can exist probabilistically, the probabilities are fixed. (I discuss stochastic determinism below.)

3. Even if such genuine randomness exists, it does not imply free will. Indeed, it is antithetical to it.

The third point is the most telling. How can an action be simultaneously random and the product of deliberative free will? Imagine a neural network in a dog. Suppose one applies a stimulus and the effect is the dog barking. The stimulus stimulates a receptor nerve or nerves (for example, the auditory nerves) and then travels deterministically along a neural path, ultimately stimulating a complex of muscles, leading to a bark. Accordingly, the stimulus leads deterministically to the response. There is no free will. Now, let us interrupt this path with a randomizing neuron. (I am just making this up. There is no evidence that such a neuron can exist.) This neuron, suppose, randomly interrupts the signal. Sometimes it goes through and the dog barks. Sometimes it does not. Is there any sense that the insertion of this random neuron in the causal chain results in free will?

Some Definitions

To facilitate the discussion in the rest of the book, I am going to use the following definitions:

Causal Determinism: The view that all events are caused. Thus, the universe has been and will be completely determined from at least the time of the big bang.

Stochastic Determinism: The view that all events are either caused or random. That is, there may exist some events, such as quantum events, that are truly random. Thus, if we reran the universe from any given point it could unfold in different ways. Nevertheless, there are only two types of events, those that are caused and those that are random.

Strong Stochastic Determinism: The view that all events are either caused or random and the conviction that random events exist, such as hypothesized by quantum mechanics. This view is also known as *indeterminism.*

Weak Stochastic Determinism: The view that all events are either caused or random. There may or may not be truly random events. (The jury is out.)

Determinism: I am going to use the general term *determinism* to describe both causal determinism and stochastic determinism. By this definition, if one says that determinism is true, this means that either causal determinism or stochastic determinism in one of its forms is true. This is a broader definition of determinism than exists in much of the literature, but since causal determinists and stochastic determinists approach the free will question similarly, it makes sense.

Afreeism

As I indicated in the Introduction, I will use the word *freeism* (free'-izm) for the belief in free will and *freeist* for someone who believes in free will. Again, I am going to define an *afreeist* (ay'-free-ist) as someone who does not have a belief in free will.

For now, here is where we stand. As we look at the universe and see it unfold, we see events as caused by other events, with the possibility of randomness at the subatomic level. Indeed, no event has ever been observed that is anything but caused or random. Neither caused nor random events form the basis of free will. The (causally or stochastically) deterministic universe is the best model of the universe that we have, the one that is supported by evidence. There is no indication that animals in general or humans in particular are somehow exempt from the laws of physics, chemistry, or other laws of the universe. Thus, there is no evidence that free will exists.

However, this is not the end of the story. First, I must acknowledge that the debate over free will is a bit more complicated than outlined above. For example, some philosophers believe that free will can exist in a deterministic universe. This may not seem possible; how can a decision be the product of free will when it was completely determined by factors existing a long time before the decision was ever made, even before the decision-maker was born? Nevertheless, the arguments of these philosophers are interesting, and we owe it to ourselves to consider them. We do so in Chapter 6.

The most interesting aspect of afreeism, however, is what it implies. What does it tell us about human autonomy, that is, our conception of ourselves as free and independent actors? What does it tell us about moral responsibility and the consequences for right and wrong? And what does it tell us about how we should live our lives, how we should treat one another, and how we should treat ourselves? These are the big questions.

For some, the implications of an absence of free will are unacceptable. A world without free will looks terrible. As a result, some philosophers have labored mightily to say that it just ain't so, that free will must exist. (I look at these efforts in Chapters 6 and 7.) But the world is what it is, irrespective of what we would like it to be. If the implications are terrible, we will just have to live with them.

I hope to convince you, however, that living life without the illusion of free will is not so bad. Indeed, I am convinced that jettisoning the belief in free will can lead to a better society and a better life. Without the illusion of free will, we can better design social policies, we can treat others better in our personal lives, and we can live more joyfully. These, I know, are strong claims. Before we get to the chapters that directly address these issues, there is a bit more work to do. I hope that you are intrigued enough to read on.

Appendix

Consciousness and Free Will

For some, free will implies the ability to make a conscious decision. Unconscious decisions, as this line of thinking goes, cannot be an exercise of free will. Some studies have indicated that some decisions that we believe to be conscious decisions are unconscious decisions. This line of studies was pioneered by neuroscientist Benjamin Libet. Here is a succinct description of his work by Joshua Shepherd:

> Libet had participants decide to flex a wrist while watching a clock and paying attention to the moment they felt an urge to flex. At the same time, Libet monitored electrical activity in the brains of participants. On average, participants reported feeling the urge to flex about 200 milliseconds before they began flexing. This is not that interesting. What was interesting was something happening in participants' brains before they felt the urge. At about 550 milliseconds before participants began flexing, electrical activity associated with voluntary action preparation began to emerge.[12]

In one interpretation of this, the brain has decided to flex before the subject reports making a conscious decision to flex.

To some, the above experiment is evidence of the lack of free will. However, Shepherd points out several critiques of this interpretation. First, discovering that the brain may be deceiving itself in some cases does not mean it is doing so for all cases. Second, it is not clear that the brain made a decision when the brain activity was first detected. Perhaps it was just preparing to make a decision.

These studies are interesting, but their importance to the debate on free will is overstated. The reason is this: decisions are determined by causal factors *whether or not* the decisions are conscious. It seems reasonable that unconscious decisions cannot be the result of free will. However, conscious decisions are equally the result of the causal chain involving the firing of neurons in reaction to other neurons and outside stimuli. As with all causal chains, this one goes back to long before the subject was born. Thus, conscious decisions cannot be the product of free will any more than unconscious decisions can be.

Chapter 2

Personal Autonomy and Decision-Making

THE ARGUMENTS FOR AFREEISM are simple: events are caused and we humans are not exempt from the laws of physics and causation. Thus events, including human choices, are determined. On the other hand, the implications of afreeism are not so clear. First, afreeism challenges our sense of personal autonomy. Second, an absence of free will implies an absence of moral responsibility for past actions. I discuss moral responsibility in Chapters 3 and 4. In the present chapter and the next, I address the issue of personal autonomy and how we make decisions in a universe where all actions and outcomes are determined.

Personal autonomy is the sense that we are free and independent agents—that we can govern ourselves. We do what we want. We weigh our options and we make decisions. The Oxford English Dictionary defines it this way:

> More generally: liberty to follow one's will; control over one's own affairs; freedom from external influence, personal independence.

AFREEISM

The Cambridge dictionary defines it as . . .

> . . . the ability to make your own decisions without being controlled by anyone else.

And Merriam-Webster describes autonomy as . . .

> . . . self-directing freedom and especially moral independence.

Afreeism throws doubt on all of this. Are we not just actors reciting our prescribed lines in a play that was written eons ago? And, if so, how much personal autonomy could we possibly have? What might our actions—indeed, our lives—signify if we are not their authors? One is reminded of this famous passage of Shakespeare:

> Life's but a walking shadow, a poor player
> That struts and frets his hour upon the stage
> And then is heard no more. It is a tale
> Told by an idiot, full of sound and fury,
> Signifying nothing.[13]

This is completely contrary to how we typically view ourselves. We prefer to think of ourselves as autonomous individuals, rather than merely actors reciting prewritten lines.

Autonomy implies that we can freely make choices. But what does it mean even to have alternatives, if only one of the so-called alternatives is ever possible? What does it mean to make a decision?

Afreeism also questions other related concepts. For example, what is the function of probability in a world where every action and every event either must happen (probability = 1) or cannot happen (probability = 0). What role can probability have in decision-making? What is the meaning of freedom, of obligation, of consent?

Communication also comes into question. For example, this book is full of statements of this sort: "If you understand the deterministic nature of the universe, you will act in ways that bring you greater joy." But what sense does it make for me to urge you to adopt a different viewpoint if everything is determined, including your viewpoint?

Finally, what role does emotion play in life and in influencing our decisions?

At the very least, once we eliminate the illusion of free will, we must look at some very common concepts quite differently. That is what this chapter explores.

Robot World

One way to begin thinking about these concepts and what they mean is to imagine a world completely populated by robots. Robots are completely determined, although in some ways they are human-like machines. Robots can do many of the same things that humans do. Some things they can do better; others, not as well. It is conceivable that one day we will develop robots of such complexity that they will achieve consciousness and be able to feel and express emotion. Perhaps the only thing that distinguishes humans from robots is their complexity.

As a mental experiment, let us create Robot World, populate it with robots, and examine how it might work. More specifically, our robots will have sensors that allow them to receive visual, auditory, and other information, much in the same way humans do through the various senses. We will give them the ability to take various actions and to move about. Finally, we will program our robots with algorithms for processing information and converting this information into action. Once we populate Robot World with our robots, we will stand back and observe how it operates. We will not intervene or control our robots. We simply want to see what they do. We are like the deist god. We set things in motion and then step aside.

Robot World, like ours, is completely deterministic. Given the initial set of inputs, the initial states of our robots, and the algorithms that our robots possess, events and actions will unfold deterministically. Concepts that make sense in Robot World should make sense in ours.

Alternatives and Decisions

Our robots will face alternatives and make decisions. Using its algorithm, a robot will weigh many factors, will calculate outcomes, and will make decisions by choosing the action that maximizes whatever goal we have specified in its algorithm.

For example, consider a robot who comes to a fork in the road. The robot must go left or go right. It cannot do both. We call left and right *alternatives*. Our robot must *choose* between the two alternatives.

In general, we define an alternative as an action that depends on the algorithm internal to the robot. That is, suppose that:

Given an external input set I and an internal algorithm A, the robot would choose action X.

Given the same external input set I and some other internal algorithm B, the robot would choose action Y.

If X and Y are different actions, then we call X and Y alternatives. If different internal algorithms would lead to different actions, then we label the different actions as alternatives.

Of course, it is completely determined which algorithm the robot possesses and therefore which alternative the robot will choose. Thus the robot is not exercising free will. However, once the robot acts, we say that the robot made a decision, even though that decision was completely determined.

Throughout this book, we will use the terms *alternative, decision, choose,* and similar terms in the way described above. All of these terms make sense in Robot World and therefore in our world.

The ability to process inputs, to deliberate, and to make decisions is a key attribute of autonomy. If we were to put a robot in a house, the robot could decide whether it chooses to go outside for a walk in the fresh air or to remain inside. Different robots, with different internal algorithms, would choose differently. If instead we put the robot in a jail, the robot would not have the freedom to go outside. In other words, regardless of its internal decision-making algorithm, the robot cannot leave its cell. In this case, the robot has less autonomy than in the first.

Ultimately, autonomy involves external constraints. Imagine putting robots with a variety of different decision-making algorithms in the same situation. Let us now impose an external constraint. If we notice some of the robots bumping into that constraint, then we can conclude that the external constraint restricts autonomy.

One might ponder at this point this old philosophical conundrum: if a deer is enclosed by a fence in the forest but in its entire life never comes upon the fence, is the deer free? (We could ask the same question about our robots.) One way to answer this question is to objectively acknowledge the restriction on movement, since other deer and robots would bump into this constraint, but also to conclude that this particular deer undoubtedly may feel free, if deer do experience this sort of emotion. Many might even conclude that this particular deer *is* free.

Fortunately, we do not have to resolve the conundrum now. We can still conclude that there may be circumstances where deer (and robots) have autonomy and circumstances where they do not.

Probability

Autonomy is all about making decisions, so we now dive into a host of issues that involve decision-making. These include the role of probability, the role of communication, and the role of emotion. Let us begin with probability.

In a deterministic world, everything that happens must happen, at least on the macro level. (As indicated in Chapter 1, there might be true random events at the subatomic level, even though this has been given a stiff challenge in recent thinking. Let us for the moment disregard subatomic quantum events for now and focus on the macro level.) The macro universe unfolds as it must. Events that happen had to happen. Decisions that are made had to be made. Alternatives that are chosen had to be chosen. Those that do not happen, could not have happened. In a sense, events that happen do so with a probability of one. Those that do not happen do so with a probability of zero.

There is, however, another sense of what probability means. Consider our robots again. Suppose that a robot is designed to collect eggs and to maximize the number of eggs it collects. It approaches a fork in the road. Suppose that it has time to go down only one of the roads. There are eggs at the end of one road, but not the other. The robot does not know which road leads to the eggs. What is a robot to do?

Well, suppose that we programmed the robot to learn and to use its knowledge to make decisions. It turns out that the robot has come to many forks. Suppose that it has turned left 100 times and right 100 times. When it has turned left, it has found eggs 85 times. When it has turned right, it has found eggs 23 times. The robot processes this information with its algorithm and turns left.

One way we can conceptualize this is to say that, given the information that the robot has, there is an 85% chance of eggs at the end of the left road and a 23% chance of eggs at the end of the right road. Suppose that we, the designers of this game, know that there are eggs at the end of the left road, but not the right. We can, with our perfect knowledge, say that there is a 100% chance of eggs at the end of the left road, and of course, that is true. The robot, however, does not have the information that we do. The robot assesses that there is an 85% chance of eggs at the end of the left road and uses this probability to make a decision.

Probabilities therefore represent a state of knowledge. As long as we understand this, it makes sense to talk about probability in a deterministic world.

Communication

We are now at a point where we can examine how robots (and therefore humans) communicate with one another. Do statements of the sort, "If you understand the deterministic nature of the universe, you will act in ways that bring you greater joy" or "I believe that you should major in philosophy" make sense in a world where all actions and outcomes are determined?

Declarative Statements, Questions, and Responses

Suppose that we have given our robots the ability to communicate with one another. One type of statement that a robot can make is a declaration of fact. One robot can communicate to another robot, "You are walking towards a cliff." The second robot can use this information to alter its behavior. Robots can also elicit information from other robots by asking questions and seeking input.

Declarative statements, questions, and responses are useful. They allow our robots to share information and to make better decisions. Likewise in our world. For example, the declarative statement, "The universe is almost certainly deterministic and therefore lacks free will," may help you make better decisions about how you treat other people and about how you treat yourself. I will have a lot to say about this in future chapters. Thus, even in a deterministic world, it makes sense to read this book.

Conditional Statements

Conditional statements are those that show dependency. Examples are:

If I study hard, I will pass the test.

If Mary were coming, she would have said something.

If Pablo had gone the other way, he would have arrived sooner.

Conditional statements do not have to represent what actually happens or happened. Indeed, they rarely do. The first two statements above represent events that may or may not happen. According to the first statement, I may study hard and pass the test, or I may not. The second statement expresses a presumption that Mary is not coming (otherwise she would have said something), although it is still possible for Mary to come. The last statement is counter-factual: Pablo did not go the other way and did not arrive sooner.

In effect, conditional statements are statements about relationships. In Robot World, these relationships may be important inputs to their decision-making algorithms. For example, in Robot World the conditional statement, "If you move two steps forward, you will fall off a cliff," may be an important input to the robot's decision as to whether to move forward.

In designing our Robot World, it would be useful for robots to communicate conditional statements to one another. The same is true for our deterministic world. Thus, the conditional statement, "If you understand the deterministic nature of the universe, you will act in ways that bring you greater joy," could (if true) be useful to you. Even though the world is deterministic.

Commands

Commands, also known as imperatives, are also useful. They are instructions. Examples:

Go to bed!

Pick up your clothes!

Do not walk on the grass!

Commands can also be linked to conditions:

If you come to a fork in the road, turn right.

If ten minutes have passed, flip the burger.

In Robot World, there are two contexts in which commands are important. First, robot programming—and, indeed, all computer programming—is just a set of commands. We can look at these at various levels of specificity. In computer programming, each line of code represents instructions to the machine. At a more general level, we can group coding into higher-level rules that the robot is programmed to carry out.

One such set of higher-level rules was envisioned by science fiction author Isaac Asimov in his short story "Runaround," which appeared later in his collection *I, Robot*. In it, Asimov poses the Three Laws of Robotics, which are:

> A robot may not injure a human being or, through inaction, allow a human being to come to harm.

> A robot must obey the orders given it by human beings except where such orders would conflict with the First Law.

> A robot must protect its own existence as long as such protection does not conflict with the First or Second Laws.

These laws were made part of each robot's coding. These laws, as envisioned by Asimov, were superior to any other conflicting commands that a robot might have.

We could also program our robots to issue commands to one another and to respond to those commands. For example, we could program our robots to shout "Stop!" if they observe another robot about to go off a cliff. We could then program our robots to stop when they hear the command "Stop!"

The above commands are simple direct commands. Some commands are just conditional statements. For example, "Stop or I will shoot!" is just a conditional statement meaning, "If you do not stop, then I will shoot you."

One robot could issue such a statement to another robot. We could program our robots to react in specific ways to such statements. Or we could program them to learn the best responses to various types of commands through the robot's own direct experience or through its observations of other robots (such as seeing another robot getting shot).

Sometimes our robots might receive conflicting commands or commands that conflict with the robot's internal commands. We would have to have a mechanism for resolving such conflicts include within the robot's algorithm. Nevertheless, providing our robots with the ability to issue and process commands could be quite useful in coordinating social behavior in Robot World.

In short, Robot World would look a lot like ours. Indeed, if complex enough, it would be indistinguishable from ours.

But What About Love?

A human characteristic closely related to human autonomy is the human ability to emote. This explains some of the resistance to accepting the deterministic nature of the world. We used the analogy of Robot World to demonstrate that the ability to reason and to make decisions makes sense in a deterministic universe. However, if we are simply complicated robots, what does this say about our ability to emote, to fall in love, to rise up in anger, to bond in friendship?

Of course, neuroscientists understand that emotions of these sorts are neurological phenomena and are thus subject to the usual rules of causation. (Because of this, one day we may even be able to design robots that experience emotion.) In short, we fall in love because our neurons fire just so.

Does this make the experience any less wonderful? Does the fact that we were determined to fall in love invalidate our experience?

In a deterministic world—the one we live in—who we love and how we love, has all been determined. My wife, for example, has not chosen to love me of her own free will. That she loves me, was determined long before either of us were born. Should that bother me? Perhaps. But it does not. Indeed, love by free will seems so calculating. Did she draw up a list, pros on one side, cons on the other? No, she was fated to love me from the day she was born.

Indeed, romantic love is often described this way. It was destined to be. As soon as she walked into the room, I had no choice but to love her. Here it is expressed in song:

It Had to Be You (Frank Sinatra)
For nobody else gave me a thrill
With all your faults, I love you still
It had to be you, wonderful you
It had to be you

Can't Help Falling in Love (Elvis Presley)
Like a river flows surely to the sea
Darling so it goes
Some things are meant to be
Take my hand, take my whole life too
For I can't help falling in love with you

No Choice in the Matter (Jason Isbell)
Love leaves you no choice in the matter
And there ain't a damn thing sadder

I Was Born to Love You (Queen)
I was born to love you
With every single beat of my heart
Yes, I was born to take care of you
Every single day of my life

i love you (Billie Eilish)
You didn't mean to say "I love you"
I love you and I don't want to

Romantic love is not a matter of choice. It makes sense in a deterministic world. Likewise, anger, anxiety, worry, hate, friendship, empathy, and kindness are all neurological phenomena that can—and do—exist in the deterministic world. Such emotions can, do, and should affect decision-making.

Indeed, understanding that the universe is deterministic could have a profound effect on our emotions and on the kind of decisions we make. Once we understand the deterministic nature of the universe, we will be less prone to judging others and more likely to accept them. We will be less prone to anger and will be less likely to feel regret, remorse, or guilt. I will discuss this more in Part III.

Autonomy in the Determinist Universe

Notice what we have done with our robot thought experiment. We have created a society of so-called autonomous robots. Once we construct Robot World, we can step back and watch it operate. The robots receive inputs and make decisions. They communicate with one another through declarative statements, conditional statements, questions, and commands. They organize their society and create rules for living.

Still, everything is caused and what happens is therefore completely determined. If we know all the algorithms and the beginning set of inputs, then we should be able to predict every single action and every single utterance of our robots. They have no free will. Of course, if we populate our

Robot World with too many robots the level of complexity may make such prediction difficult. Nevertheless, Robot World is completely deterministic.

We say that our robots are "autonomous" (in a sense) because they can deliberate, make decisions, and act accordingly, even though everything they do is determined. Their decisions, although determined, determine the outcome of their history and the course of their world.

That said, we need to recognize that 1) the very concept of autonomy is not well defined and is subject to philosophical debate, and 2) there may be different levels or even types of autonomy. For the purpose of our discussion, we can begin with a robot who faces a decision. That decision is completely determined by the internal algorithm of the robot and the inputs to that algorithm. We can then ask what would happen if the robot had an alternative internal algorithm. We could do this for a large number of algorithms, noticing each time what decision the robot would make.

If all internal algorithms lead to the same decision, then the robot is not acting autonomously. If the range of internal algorithms leads to a wide range of decisions, then the robot is acting with a lot of autonomy. If the same range of algorithms would lead to a narrow set of decisions, then we say that there is less autonomy.

By this definition of autonomy, robots (and humans) have more autonomy if they have fewer physical limitations on their behavior or fewer negative consequences to their actions. For example, removing penalties for political action can increase autonomy. So can removing negative consequences of decisions affecting reproduction. Autonomy is also increased when we give access—through ramps, elevators, and the like—to those who are wheelchair-bound.

This, of course, does not answer all (or even most) of the questions about what constitutes autonomy and what does not. Nevertheless, it does answer one question: can autonomy exist in our deterministic universe? It does. Autonomy without free will.

Chapter 3

Moral Obligation

WITH OUR DISCUSSION in Chapter 2, we now have the tools to discuss moral obligation (this chapter) and moral responsibility (Chapter 4). What does moral obligation mean? Indeed, what does any sort of obligation mean?

Obligation

Before we tackle moral obligation, we need to know what we mean by obligation *writ large*. The problem with the concept of obligation, given that the world is deterministic, is that we are obligated by causal forces to do *everything* that we do. But if every action is obligated, then the concept of obligation loses its meaning and usefulness. If "to obligate" just means "to cause," then the term "obligate" adds nothing to our vocabulary. Therefore, for the concept of obligation to be useful, it cannot just refer to actions that are caused.

Legal Obligation

Fortunately, obligation has other meanings that make sense in a deterministic world. As an example, consider *legal obligation* as expressed in this statement:

> You have a legal obligation to file your taxes by the dead-line.

This seems simple enough. The word *legal* refers to the government. This says that if you do not file your taxes by the deadline, then there will be legal consequences. That is, you may be required to pay a fine, and if you are particularly stubborn, you might even find yourself in jail. Note that you may still decline to file your taxes by the deadline and accept the consequences. Therefore, if we define obligation as simply a specific type of conditional statement, then it makes perfect sense in a deterministic world. We could rewrite the above statement, for example, as:

> If you do not file your taxes on time, the government will fine you $1000.

What makes this a legal obligation is that the first part of the conditional statement refers to an action (or inaction) and the second part of the conditional statement is a government-imposed sanction. Thusly defined, we can note the following about this sort of obligation:

1. Not all acts are subject to a legal obligation, and

2. Those acts subject to a legal obligation may nevertheless not happen.

Thus, legal obligation means something quite different from causation.

Moral Obligation

Moral obligation also makes sense in a deterministic world. Consider the following statement:

> You have a moral obligation to contribute to the support of your children.

Note that you may or may not have a legal obligation to care for your children, depending on the circumstances, but in either case, someone could make the claim that you have a moral obligation to do so. Religious and philosophical traditions posit all sorts of moral obligations, from the Ten Commandments to the Golden Rule to the Eight Fold Path to the Ten Vedic Restraints to the precepts of Confucius and on and on. Such moral obligations are typically not expressed conditionally, but rather as commands:

> Thou shall not kill.

> Hate not.

> Practice noninjury.

As we noted in Chapter 2, commands make perfect sense in a deterministic universe. We could, for example, program our robots with various moral obligations. (Again, note Asimov's Three Laws of Robotics.)

Moral Rules

We typically express moral obligation as moral rules. Moral rules characterize certain kinds of behavior as either good or bad. At its root, moral philosophy seeks to identify what kinds of behavior are good and what kinds of behavior are bad.

There are many sources of moral rules. Some believe that the question of good and evil is answered by canonical texts. Good and bad behaviors are what the Bible, the Quran, the Book of Mormon, or the Hindu texts say they are. Or perhaps they are expressed by the utterances of a charismatic or spiritual leader.

Afreeism does not answer the question of what behavior is good or what behavior is bad. Because afreeism is based in science rather than faith, its adherents are more likely to take a nondogmatic approach. That is, afreeists are likely to define good behaviors as those that promote flourishing and bad behaviors as those that cause suffering. Some candidates for moral rules along these lines might include some of the rules our parents taught us:[14]

> **Reciprocity** (also known as the Golden Rule): Treat others as you would like to be treated. (Parent: "How would you feel if someone did that to you?") Versions of this rule date at least from the time of Confucius.

> **Universality** (also known as Kant's Categorical Imperative): Adopt a moral rule if and only if you would have that moral rule become a universal law. (Parent: "What if everyone acted like that?")

To this, I would add one more:

> **The Veil of Ignorance:** This idea was developed by the philosopher John Rawls.[15] It goes like this: in adopting a moral (societal) rule, pretend that you do not know which member of society you will be. Would you adopt this rule under these circumstances? (This is sort of like the "I cut, you choose" rule for divvying up desserts.)

Of course, these rules do not answer many of the hard moral questions. Afreeists must struggle with these as do other thinkers.

Moral rules are completely compatible with determinism. As we saw in Robot World, we could program our robots to follow moral rules. Or we could program them to create their own. Most likely, the rules we would choose would be ones that allow the society to function and its inhabitants to flourish.

Indeed, if we are sufficiently clever and good enough programmers, we could program our robots to create their own internal commands. For example, we could program our robots to adopt internal commands that satisfy a specified criterion. Here is an example of a criterion inspired by Kant's categorical imperative:

> A robot will adopt an internal command if the robot determines that Robot World would be better off if all robots adopted the command.

Of course, we would have to program the robot to know what "better" meant in the above question. This would involve having some type of social welfare function that our robots could reference.

Moral Obligation and Afreeism

Moral obligation makes perfect sense in a deterministic universe. Moral rules would likely make both robot and human society function better. Moral obligation is completely compatible with afreeism. But not so for moral responsibility. That is the topic of the next chapter.

Chapter 4

Moral Responsibility

MORAL RESPONSIBILITY IS PERHAPS the *raison d'être* of the free will debate. (This will become very apparent in Chapters 5 and 6.) This is not to say that it is the only issue. However, without the issue of moral responsibility, no one would likely care much about free will. The argument goes like this: if people do not have free will, how can we hold them morally responsible for actions that they have taken? And without moral responsibility, what becomes of human behavior? Why would anyone act morally if we do not hold them accountable?

Moral responsibility is tied to the idea of desert. The noun *desert* refers to the concept of deserving. It also signifies that which is deserved. If one receives her just deserts, she is getting what she deserves. To say that a person is morally responsible for an action is to say that they deserve punishment or reward for having taken that action.

The Nature of Moral Responsibility

Free will is a physical phenomenon, which is to say that whether it exists or not depends on how the physical laws of the universe work. Free will can exist only if people have the physical ability to do otherwise from what they do. Since they do not, free will cannot exist.

Moral responsibility is different. Moral responsibility is a social and psychological construct. This is to say that people are morally responsible for their past actions only if we (society) say and feel that they are. The question is whether it makes sense to say that people are morally responsible for actions that they have taken.

Desert

Because both desert and moral responsibility mean various things in the English language, I want to be clear what we mean here by each. Let us begin with desert.

Sometimes we reward a person after some good behavior or punish her after bad behavior. We justify these rewards and punishments in various ways. Consider two different justifications:

> **Desert:** We punish Person X because she deserves to be punished for committing a bad act. We reward Person X because she deserves to be rewarded for committing some good act.

> **Incentives:** We punish Person X to deter her and others from committing the bad act in the future. We reward Person X to encourage her and others to do similar acts in the future.

So desert means something distinct from creating incentives. The following statements are expressions of desert:

The driver of a getaway car in a bank robbery deserves a five-year prison sentence.

The salesperson who worked hard and produced a good sales record deserves a promotion.

The word *deserve* has other uses in the English language as well, and this sometimes leads to confusion. For example, consider these statements:

The sick child deserves care and medical attention.

The beautiful building deserves to be preserved.

The poor guy deserves a bit of good luck.

The American public deserves good government.

These uses of the word *deserve* are different than the two previously mentioned uses because they do not involve punishments or rewards, at least not explicitly, and are not tied to any particular action. I will not be using *deserve* in these ways. For our purposes, *deserve* will mean the appropriateness of receiving a reward (or punishment) simply because an action is good (or bad) and the actor chose to do it.

In contrast to the notion of desert, rewards and punishment can instead be based on incentives. Using the incentive justification, we punish or reward people to affect their future actions and the future actions of others.

Sometimes we justify a consequence based on both desert and incentives. For example, we may say that the punishment for murder may be deserved and may also serve to deter. Other consequences may be justified on deterrence alone. For example, some cities have enacted congestion fees for driving in the city during certain high-traffic hours. The car is fitted with a transponder and if the car enters the controlled zone, the driver's credit card is charged. This is designed to deter driving to reduce congestion. Nevertheless, we do not pass moral judgment on someone who drives in the city during the specified hours. She is simply choosing to do so and accepts the price. Likewise, we may justify some consequences on desert alone. Some would say, for example, that a thief deserves to be punished even if the punishment had absolutely no deterrent effect.

Note that consequences may have other rationales as well. The government may impose monetary consequences for actions simply to raise revenue. For example, a tax for fishing (through the sale of fishing licenses) may serve simply to raise revenue to pay for fish management. In addition, we may isolate a dangerously violent person or quarantine the carrier of an infectious disease merely to remove them from society, thereby protecting its citizens.

One way to determine whether a punishment or reward is based on desert is to ask the following question: if we eliminate all other rationales, do we still feel that the person should be rewarded or punished? For example, if we are convinced that the consequence would not deter, would not raise revenue, would not protect the public through isolation, etc., do we still believe that the person should be punished? If we answer yes, we are probably basing our consequence on desert alone.

Moral Responsibility

Moral responsibility is just another way of expressing the idea of desert. Consider the following statement:

The driver who drove the getaway car in the bank robbery is morally responsible for her action.

This statement is just saying that the driver deserves punishment. Along the same lines, philosopher Derk Pereboom defines moral responsibility as follows:

[F]or an agent to be morally responsible for an action is for it to belong to her in such a way that she would deserve blame if she understood that it was morally wrong, and she would deserve credit or perhaps praise if she understood that it was morally exemplary.[16]

When philosophers talk about moral responsibility, it is this sort of definition that they typically have in mind. According to the definition, someone is morally responsible for an action if she deserves blame or credit for the action.

That said, moral responsibility is sometimes used in a different sense, which is simply to acknowledge the existence of a moral rule. Consider this statement:

Parents have a moral responsibility to give their children a good education.

When moral responsibility is used this way, it means moral obligation. So, we could say:

Parents have a moral obligation to give their children a good education.

Or,

Parents should give their children a good education.

This simply expresses a moral rule. It says nothing about the consequences of failing to abide by it. Some philosophers will claim that a rule is not a rule without an enforcement mechanism. John Stuart Mill was of this mind. He writes:

We do not call anything wrong unless we mean to imply that a person ought to be punished in some way for doing it—if not by law, by the opinion of his fellow creatures; if not by opinion, by the reproaches of his own conscience.

However, there is no reason why a rule requires punishment to enforce it. For example, we could program our robots in Robot World to follow certain moral rules. They would do so, even without punishment.

The Psychology of Desert

Above I stated that people are morally responsible for their past actions only if we (society) say and feel that they are. Feeling is an important aspect of desert. When we believe that people deserve something, it just feels good when they get it. Such feelings have deep evolutionary roots. (I discuss this in greater detail in Chapter 10.)

However, punishment feels good only if we believe that the person who receives the punishment deserves it. Punishing the wrong person, or punishing someone who could not have done otherwise, brings no pleasure at all. We do not get pleasure from seeing someone punished who was caused to do the act because of an epileptic seizure or a brain tumor.

The Argument

Although desert and moral responsibility are social and psychological phenomena, they depend on the physical phenomenon of free will, that is, on the ability to do otherwise. Without free will, or the ability to do otherwise, the concepts of desert and moral responsibility have no application. In what follows, I am going to argue that no person is ever morally responsible for actions taken. That is, no person ever deserves reward or punishment. More precisely, the reasoning is this:

Premise 1: A person deserves the consequences of her actions only if she could have done otherwise. If she could not have done otherwise, then she cannot deserve what happens as a result.

Premise 2: Since the universe is deterministic, no person could have done other than what she did.

Conclusion: Thus a person never deserves the consequences of her actions; no person ever deserves punishment or reward. That is, no person is ever morally responsible for an action that she has taken.

In what follows, I will give a more detailed explanation of the above and will explore some of the implications of this argument.

The Ability To Do Otherwise

For someone to deserve a punishment or reward, she has to have the ability to make a free choice. Sometimes we express this as follows:[17]

A person deserves a consequence (a desert), only if,

1. The person committed the act.

2. The act had some moral character. That is, the act was either good or bad.

3. The person knew or should have known the moral character of the act. That is, if the act was morally wrong, the person knew or should have known that the act was morally wrong. If it was exemplary, then the person knew that.

4. The person could have done otherwise.

Without these conditions, there is no desert. Indeed, this is another way to identify whether we are basing a consequence on desert or on some other justification. We ask the following question: if we were to learn that the person had to do what they did, that they could not have done otherwise, would we still want to punish or reward her?

I should note that these are minimal conditions. Some situations satisfy these conditions and yet there is still no desert. For example, a driver who is speeding because a carjacker is holding a gun to her head satisfies these conditions because technically the driver could have refused to speed and risked getting shot. Yet we would not say that a driver who speeds in these circumstances deserves punishment.

The ability to do otherwise is key to desert. If a person could not do otherwise, then she cannot deserve punishment or reward. A few thought experiments will confirm this. Consider three scenarios:

1. A person pulls the trigger and kills someone out of a desire to collect the victim's life insurance.

2. A person who is examining a gun pulls the trigger and kills someone as the result of a seizure caused by a heretofore-unknown brain tumor.

3. During brain surgery to remove a benign tumor, an evil neurosurgeon secretly implants an electrode in the brain of a subject. When triggered, the electrode creates an irresistible desire in the subject to kill the first person she sees. The evil neurosurgeon triggers the electrode and the subject kills the person in the room with her at the time.

In the second case, most people have no problem concluding that the subject does not deserve punishment. The reason is that the subject could not have done otherwise. In the third case, where the subject did what she wanted to do, her irresistible desire was created by the neurosurgeon so that her choice was inevitable. Again, no desert.

What many people do not realize, however, is that the first case is the same as the other two. Even in the first case, a causal chain results in events unfolding in only one possible way. So in the deterministic universe (the one in which we live), there is no justification for desert, as we have defined it, in any of the three cases. The fourth condition outlined above is never satisfied.

I should mention that some philosophers have argued that desert exists even in a deterministic universe. To make this fit, they have had to abandon condition 4 above, that one has to have the ability to do otherwise. They would like to say that a person deserves punishment in the first case but not in the other two. But since they concede that the actor could not have done otherwise in any of the three cases, how do they distinguish the first case from the other two? No one has ever succeeded in explaining why, but the attempts are very instructive. We examine such arguments in Chapter 6.

Robot World Revisited

We might ask this question: even if desert for past actions does not make much sense, should we nevertheless embrace it for the pragmatic reasons of modifying future behavior? For example, we could program our robots as follows:

1. We program into our robots the notion of desert that we specified above. They would then punish or reward an act only if they perceived that the actor had the ability to do otherwise.

2. We program our robots to (falsely) believe that, for some actions (those we want to modify), there is an ability to do otherwise. That is, we deceive them into believing that free will exists. (We must also give our robots some algorithm for labeling some actions as the product of free will and others not.)

There are several difficulties with this second step. Because we know that there is never an ability to do otherwise, it is unclear how we can program our robots to identify actions where they would apply desert. We would need to trick our robots into dividing actions into those where there is an ability to do otherwise and others where there is no such ability. To do so, we would need some other criteria that would do the dividing while making our robots believe that it is based on the ability to do otherwise.

The question is whether it is useful to go through this charade. There are several problems with this approach. First, if we make our robots rational enough, they will soon discover that their world is deterministic and therefore that there is never an ability to do otherwise. That is, they will see through the charade. (As we are seeing through it!) Thus they would never apply rewards or punishment based on desert.

Second, it is unnecessary. Indeed, if the reason we are giving our robots such algorithms is to modify future behavior, then what we are truly interested in are incentives (and deterrents). Why not simply program our robots to recognize good and bad behavior and endow them with the ability to apply rewards and punishments to encourage or deter? That is, why not base punishment and rewards directly on incentives and not on desert.

Finally, deceiving our robots into believing in desert is counterproductive. Even if we do manage to trick our robots into believing that there is sometimes the ability to do otherwise, we may find our robots punishing and rewarding where the punishment or reward does little or nothing to modify behavior. Or they may punish too much or too little. Indeed, in the human world people apply or support the application of inhumane and ineffective punishments on the basis of desert (retribution). In these cases, the amount of suffering may substantially outweigh the social benefit of deterrence.

Implications of Afreeism

Afreeism and its rejection of desert and moral responsibility for past actions embraces the following ideas:

1. There can be—and, in fact, there are—moral rules. (This was discussed in Chapters 2 and 3.)

2. Nevertheless, one never deserves blame, punishment, praise, or reward for any action or inaction simply because in the deterministic universe no one ever could have done otherwise.

3. There may be other ways to justify punishments and rewards.

4. Once we abandon desert as a justification, our system of punishments and rewards will likely look quite different. I will discuss this in future chapters. In brief, the severity of punishments will likely decrease. Instead, we will punish those who commit crimes more like we punish our children—to teach them and deter them, with restraint and perhaps a bit of sadness. We will also recalibrate rewards. Extremes of wealth and poverty may no longer be justified.

5. Finally, what applies to others applies to ourselves. We do not deserve punishment or rewards either. We explore the implications of this in later chapters. We will see that feelings of guilt, shame, regret, and remorse are no longer justified. Eliminating them removes impediments to joy.

Of course, there are still unresolved issues. For example, punishing a person always involves punishing someone who, in an important sense, is innocent, given that in a deterministic universe everyone is always innocent. We therefore need a theory of punishment that accepts this fact. We examine this in Chapter 10.

To summarize, afreeism holds that desert is not justified and that we are not morally responsible for past actions. This will significantly affect the way we approach the world. We will see that the rejection of the idea of desert has major implications for social policy, including how we approach the criminal law system. Discarding the concept of desert also has important repercussions for notions of freedom and regulation, income and wealth distribution, foreign policy, immigration, and affirmative action, among others. It can also affect us more personally, influencing how we treat others and ourselves. We delve into this change in perspective in the following chapter.

Chapter 5

The Lens of Causation

AS WE SAW FROM THE PREVIOUS CHAPTERS, our view of the world still makes a lot of sense even when we realize that we do not have free will. We still operate as autonomous individuals. We deliberate and make decisions, we weigh costs and benefits, we communicate with our fellow humans in the usual ways, and we take action.

Yet not everything remains the same. Some things will change. Realizing that the world is deterministic and that we have no free will makes us look at some things very differently. To understand the afreeist perspective, we must keep in mind two things:

1. The universe unfolds through a causal chain, and

2. Causation looks quite different depending on whether we are looking to the future or looking at the past.

The *lens of causation* illustrates the dual nature of causality. Imagine a landscape of time going forward into the future and backward into the past. You observe both the future and the past through this special lens—the lens of causation. What do you see? First, look forward into the future. You cannot see the future with precision through this or any other lens. Instead, roads spread out in front of you and go off into the distance. These roads fork in a seemingly infinite pattern of possibilities leading to outcomes ranging from the sublime, to the beautiful, to the mundane, to the terrifying. Sometimes you cannot see where a road is going, or you cannot see it clearly. The road may disappear over a hill, for example. But you can see many of the roads and forks. Robert Frost poetically described such a fork in the road:

> Two roads diverged in a yellow wood,
> And sorry I could not travel both
> And be one traveler, long I stood
> And looked down one as far as I could
> To where it bent in the undergrowth;
>
> Then took the other, as just as fair,
> And having perhaps the better claim,
> Because it was grassy and wanted wear;
> Though as for that the passing there
> Had worn them really about the same[18]

Some of the forks in the roads represent choices that you must make. In decision theory, these are called *choice nodes* or *decision nodes*. Other forks represent paths that could turn out one way or the other unpredictably, so-called random events. These forks are, in decision theory, *chance nodes*. We assign probabilities to the various branches of a chance node. (Recall from Chapter 2 that a probability represents a lack of knowledge and an estimate of likelihood.)

Looking forward into the future through the lens of causation, you can see that what you do makes a difference. You may not be able to predict exactly what will happen, but you can have some influence over it. Taking different roads leads to different outcomes. Due to causation, the decisions that you make will, along with other factors, determine those outcomes.

In a sense, looking at the future through the lens of causation looks a lot like what all of us do naturally. (It is also what our robots in Robot World do.) We come to decision nodes and we try to predict the outcomes from various alternatives. Because we have the knowledge and understanding that events in the universe are caused, we can make predictions, although often imperfect ones. If we know enough about the causes, we can make good predictions. If we know less, then our predictions will be worse. Nevertheless, what we do matters.

Now let us suppose that you have come to a fork—to a choice node—and you must decide whether to take one road or another. You look ahead and, using causation, try to determine how your choice will affect your life and the lives of others. You weigh your options and make a choice. You proceed down one of the roads.

Now turn around and look through the same lens of causation towards the past. It looks quite different than you remember. The beautiful pattern of possibility has disappeared. There is now only one road as far back as you can see. It is the road that you have traveled. You see no other roads. You see no forks, no crossroads. Because of causation, there was in reality only one road. There was only one action you could have taken at each choice node that you encountered.

What does this mean? First, looking ahead you see *alternatives*. (Recall that we define an alternative as an action that depends on our internal algorithms. If different internal algorithms could lead to different actions, then the various actions are called alternatives.) Because the world is causal, what you do matters. What road you take will determine (along with a host of other factors), where you end up. From your perspective, then, it is important to plan well, to research your options, and to make the best choices you can with the information you have. As part of your decision-making algorithm, you likely will consider what you value in life, your feelings and emotions, your relationships with people around you, and your philosophical view of what is the good society, among other things. (Of course, as with our robots, your algorithm is also determined. Different people will take into consideration different things.)

Again, causation implies that what you do matters. It affects your happiness and the happiness of those you care about and, in some small way perhaps, the type of world you and those who come after you will live in. That is what causation says. What you do causes a host of other events and actions stretching into the future. You are a cause. A caused cause.

However, once you have made a decision and have, so to speak, moved past that fork in the road, you will be able to turn around look at that decision in the past through that same lens of causation. All of the untaken options now have disappeared and you realize that the action that you took was the only action possible. This hindsight perspective is immensely freeing. You cannot feel guilty, ashamed, remorseful, or regretful for actions that simply had to be. Nor can you blame others for actions that they have taken. It was all determined.

Determinism versus Fatalism

Still, some people believe that if the world is determined, and outcomes set in stone, then it is pointless to try to improve ourselves or to improve the world. What is going to happen, will happen. This misunderstands determinism and afreeism. It is precisely because the world is causal that what we do makes a difference. Afreeism is a philosophy of action, not of futility.

One reason that some people assume that determinism implies futility is that they confuse fatalism and determinism. Fatalism says that a specific outcome is inevitable no matter what a person does. To say that I am fated to die at the age of 43, for example, is to say that, no matter what I do, no matter how well I eat, no matter how much exercise I get, no matter how many or few life-threatening activities I engage in, I will die at 43. Fatalism says that outcome C will occur irrespective of whether I take action A or action B.

This is not determinism. Because the universe is deterministic, it may be true that I will die at the age of 43, but I will do so *because* of actions that I take and because of other factors unrelated to my actions. If I had gotten more exercise, eaten better and gone to the doctor more often, then I would not have died at the age of 43. Unfortunately (for me), I could not have done otherwise than what I did. The causal chain led inevitably to me getting less exercise, eating unhealthily, avoiding my doctor, etc. Thus, although I am one of the causes of my own demise, I could not have done otherwise.

Consider this again in the context of Robot World. If we program a robot to eat healthily, exercise and get regular checkups, it will likely do better than a robot who we do not program to do these things. And it makes perfect sense for one robot to communicate this to another robot. *If you exercise, eat healthily and get regular checkups, you will live longer.* Statements such as this one can be processed by the robot algorithm. Such statements constitute inputs that could, along with other inputs, cause the robot to do these things. (It is my hope that these pages will constitute such as an input for you.)

The Asymmetry of Perspective

In short, the perspective of afreeism is asymmetric. Looking toward the future, we see that what we do matters. It benefits us to learn, to analyze, and to act. This is true even though the world is deterministic. Looking towards the past, however, we see that what we did was inevitable. We should feel no guilt, no shame, no regret, and no remorse. Indeed, there are only two reasons to look at the past at all. The first is to enjoy the good memories. The second is to learn from our past mistakes.

The Stoics of ancient Greece and Rome, who we will encounter again in later chapters, were determinists who had precisely this perspective, both looking forward to the future and looking backward to the past. As William Irving writes:

> [The Stoics] are advising us to be fatalistic with respect to the past, to keep firmly in mind that the past cannot be changed. Thus, the Stoics would not counsel a mother with a sick child to be fatalistic with respect to the future; she should try to nurse the child back to health (even though the Fates have already decided whether the child lives or dies). But if the child dies, they will counsel this woman to be fatalistic with respect to the past. It is only natural, even for Stoics, to experience grief after the death of a child. But to dwell on that death is a waste of time and emotions, inasmuch as the past cannot be changed.[19]

In the above passage, *fatalistic* should be understood to mean *deterministic*. It is interesting, but completely consistent with the Stoic acceptance of determinism, that some of the greatest Stoic philosophers were people of action. Seneca (born probably around 1-4 BCE) was a philosopher, playwright, Roman senator, and advisor to the emperor Nero. Another Stoic philosopher, Marcus Aurelius, was the emperor of Rome from 61 CE until his death in 80 CE. Like Stoicism, afreeism counsels action, looking forward. Looking to the past, it counsels acceptance and tolerance.

To summarize, causation has different implications depending on whether one is looking forward or looking backward. Looking forward through the lens of causation, we see that the future depends on what we do in each instance. It therefore benefits us to give some attention to the future. Again, this statement is true even though the world is deterministic. Looking backward through that same lens, we realize that, because of the chain of causation, what happened (including all of the decisions we made) had to happen.

This perspective, which represents our best conception of reality, can be very disconcerting at first, but ultimately feels quite liberating. It changes how we view the world.

Chapter 6

The Counterarguments (And Why They Don't Work)

THE FIRST THREE CHAPTERS LAID OUT the basic arguments as to why a faith in free will is unjustified and why moral responsibility simply does not make sense. These are easy arguments to make, but hard arguments to accept. The notions of determinism (whether causal or stochastic) and afreeism have produced a furious philosophical backlash. This is understandable. We like to believe that we are in control of ourselves. We like to believe that we are all morally responsible for our actions. Determinism, and consequently the lack of free will, threatens both of these notions. In spite of the logic of determinism, philosophers have proposed many arguments as to why free will and moral responsibility exist. We owe it to ourselves to consider these arguments. They are, for the most part, thoughtful and interesting. Ultimately, however, they are not persuasive. Furthermore, by studying these defenses of free will, we come closer to understanding why free will does not exist.

Defenses of Free Will and Moral Responsibility

Philosophers have employed several approaches to defend free will and moral responsibility. We can group these strategies into three categories:

The Libertarian Argument: The universe is not causally or stochastically deterministic and therefore humans are capable of making decisions that are not caused or random.

The Compatibilist Argument: The universe may be deterministic, but we can redefine free will so that free will and moral responsibility exist anyway.

The Consequentialist Argument: Free will and moral responsibility (or a belief in free will and moral responsibility) must exist (irrespective of determinism) because the world will be better if they do.

These are sincerely held and imaginatively argued positions. However, none of them holds up to scrutiny. Nevertheless, it is important to understand them and to understand why they fail. Let us look at each of these approaches in turn.

The Libertarian Argument: The Universe Is Not Causally or Stochastically Deterministic

Some believers in free will accept the idea that determinism and free will cannot coexist. If determinism is true, if people cannot do otherwise than what they do, then free will cannot exist. Given this, some philosophers defend the notion of free will by arguing that the world is not deterministic. That is, they argue that humans can take actions that are neither caused nor random.

Those who hold these views are known as *libertarians.* (This is not the same as the political definition of libertarianism.) A libertarian is someone who denies that the world is deterministic.

Libertarians are a type of *incompatibilist.* Incompatibilists believe that determinism and free will cannot both be true. In order to defend the idea of free will, libertarians conclude that determinism cannot be true. Other incompatibilists, discussed below, come to the opposite conclusion. That is, they conclude that determinism is true and free will therefore cannot exist.

The problem with philosophical libertarianism is that there is no good theory as to how there can exist actions that are neither caused nor random. Libertarians try to justify their claim in a variety of ways.[20] Some libertarians see the ability to take actions that are neither caused nor random as coming from the divine. Others refer to physics or neurobiology. For example, one account asserts that parallel processing in the brain in conjunction with quantum mechanics and chaos theory combine to produce actions that are neither caused nor random. Unfortunately for this claim, the science does not show this.

Most of the argumentation for the libertarian viewpoint, rather than being rooted in science, is based on philosophical models. For example, a model might assert that moral responsibility must exist, but because moral responsibility makes no sense absent free will, then free will must exist. And because free will cannot exist if the world is deterministic, the world must not be deterministic. (The tail wags the dog.)

To understand why philosophical models of free will are unconvincing, we need to consider the different ways in which we can look at phenomena. We can view phenomena from many different levels and through many different lenses or explanatory models. For example, suppose a person walks into a room and sees her romantic partner in a compromising situation. She reacts. We can model this reaction in a variety of ways:

Physics: Certain photons were refracted through the lens of the eye, hitting the back of the eye, causing certain atoms to absorb energy, exciting other atoms in the nervous system and brain, ultimately exciting protein molecules and producing a physical reaction.

Neurobiology: Light hits photosensitive neurons in the back of the eye, creating electrical impulses that get transmitted to the brain, which get processed by the amygdala of the brain, which transmits to the cerebral cortex, causing it to react through a complicated neural network, resulting in a physical reaction.

Psychology: The subject walks into a room, sees her romantic partner interacting romantically with someone else, which causes anger and brings up memories of the subject's unfaithful father, ultimately producing a physical reaction.

Sociology: Human culture has developed mechanisms for organized reproduction, which involve the creation of norms around mating, which have been internalized by members of society and which produce physical reactions under circumstances such as these.

Evolutionary Biology: Males and females evolved in a manner that encouraged the propagation of genes, which result in an instinctual response to oppose other reproductive competition.

Philosophy: The reaction of the subject can be understood and evaluated through a moral lens that posits how subjects should respond in certain situations.

We develop such models because they are useful in motivating, explaining, and predicting human behavior. Some models are better suited for answering particular questions about certain human behaviors than others. Specifically, the physics and neurobiological models give us answers to the questions of causation and determinism. Looking at events from a physics or neurobiological perspective, we observe that no event has ever been known to occur without either being caused or (for subatomic particles) being (possibly) random. Against this overwhelming evidence, libertarians present philosophical models that would require us to reject the overwhelming evidence provided by the physics and the neurobiological models. These philosophical models are simply not convincing. Most philosophers do not accept the libertarian view because it conflicts so directly with science. This is not to say that philosophical models are not useful. However, for this particular question on whether the universe is deterministic, they cannot hold a candle to the physics and neurobiological models. For other purposes, philosophical models might be quite illuminating.

Libertarians, despite having struggled mightily to prove the existence of free will and to refute determinism, have ultimately failed. For those interested in the libertarian approach, a more detailed look at these models appears in Meghan Griffith's[21] excellent book on free will.

The Compatibilist Argument: The World May Be Deterministic, But We Can Redefine Free Will So That It Still Exists

Philosophers who claim that free will can exist in a deterministic universe are known as *compatibilists.* The terminology is a bit tricky here. A compatibilist does not necessarily concede that the universe is deterministic, but says that *if* it is deterministic, free will can still exist. Philosophers who believe that the universe is indeed deterministic but also believe that free will exists are known as *soft determinists.* (Soft determinists are a subset of compatibilists.)

That said, most philosophers who call themselves compatibilists write and act as if they were soft determinists. That is, they believe that the universe is most likely deterministic and that free will exists anyway. (You may have heard the canard that an agnostic is just an atheist without conviction. In the same sense, a compatibilist is just a soft determinist without conviction.)

The primary argument for compatibilism is that humans are different from other organisms. Although everything is caused, the way it is caused in humans is different. Humans do not act the way insects act, for example. In insects, if you apply a stimulus you get a fixed and replicable response. Some human activity is like this, but other human activity is different. Humans often deliberate. Frequently, humans have reasons that justify their decisions. Reasons are forward-looking. Compatibilists call this forward-looking, reason-based decision-making free will.

The Counterarguments

The sorts of things that count for reasons also matter. Humans have moral values. These values help define who we are and are inputs into the forward-looking reason-based decision calculus. To compatibilists, all of these characteristics of human decision-making imply free will.

At bottom, compatibilists accomplish their goal of having free will exist in a deterministic universe by defining free will in such a way that free will is not negated by determinism. Recall that our working definition of free will is *the freedom of humans to make choices that are not determined by prior causes or by divine intervention.* Compatibilists reject this definition and offer other definitions of free will in its place. One simple compatibilist way to redefine free will is this:

A person exercises free will whenever that person acts according to his or her desires.

Under this definition, the fact that what a person desires is completely determined is irrelevant to the existence of free will. Therefore, even if an action is completely determined by prior events (because desires are completely determined), it still can be, according to the compatibilist, a product of free will.

The definition of free will that most compatibilists employ is more complicated and nuanced than the one I have given above. Sometimes this is stated in terms of control. If a person can exercise control, then there is free will, even though the control exercised is completely determined. Another formulation states that if the primary causes of an action are external to the individual, then there is no free will. If they are internal, then there is free will.

Along similar lines, some compatibilists try to dissect the mind and categorize types of decisions. Those that are influenced by our moral understandings are said to be free. Those that are determined by appetites, addictions, or external factors are not. This is sometimes called "source compatibilism" because it looks at the causal source within the brain that generates the decision. There are a variety of other compatibilist arguments that appear under other labels, such as *revisionism*[22] and *dispositional compatibilism*[23]. (Just for fun, in the appendix to this chapter, I present a well-known and oft-discussed compatibilist argument.)

What is true in all versions of compatibilism is that we end up with an altered definition of free will. The compatibilist arguments are ultimately unconvincing. Humans do indeed make forward-looking, reason-based, value-laden decisions. But that does not change the fact that the reasons and the values were all determined long before the person was born. There was simply no other outcome possible. If no other outcome is possible, how can this be free will in the sense that most of us understand the term?

To approach this another way we can ask: does the compatibilist version of free will exist in Robot World? The robots in Robot World make decisions based on inputs and their algorithms. We can even program them with moral rules. The moral rules may sometimes conflict with other goals, so we would have to put into the computer algorithm a way to resolve internal conflicts. Our robots make forward-looking, reason-based, value-laden decisions. So, by compatibilist standards, our robots have free will.

Nevertheless, when our robots make decisions, they do so deterministically. They can never do other than what the combination of their inputs and their algorithms dictate. Would we ever conclude that our robots have free will? Would we ever hold them morally responsible for actions that they simply had to perform?

For compatibilists, the belief in free will and moral responsibility runs up against the overwhelming evidence of determinism. Compatibilists attempt to reconcile these two ideas. They do so by changing the definition of free will to such a degree that free will is no longer recognizable. This strategy is akin to changing the definition of unicorn to simply a white horse in order to argue that unicorns exist.

Semicompatibilism

Compatibilists' semantic maneuvering allows them to define free will into existence. However, this is not their principal aim. Compatibilists want free will to exist because they want to justify holding people responsible for past actions. Some philosophers, known as *semicompatibilists*, have recognized the fact that free will is incompatible with determinism. Nevertheless, they argue that the concept of moral responsibility for past actions makes sense. What makes semicompatibilists different from compatibilists is that semicompatibilists go directly to the issue of desert and moral responsibility without getting bogged down with the idea of free will. This, in a way, is an easier approach because free will is a physical phenomenon while moral responsibility is a social construct.

Nevertheless, semicompatibilism fails for the same reason that compatibilism fails. That is, moral responsibility, even as a social construct, requires the ability to do otherwise. As always, one could try to create a definition of moral responsibility that does require the ability to do otherwise, but such a definition would no doubt be just as unrecognizable to us as the compatibilist's rebranding of the notion of free will. The better approach is just to admit that moral responsibility for past actions simply does not make sense.

The Consequentialist Argument: Free Will and Moral Responsibility (or a Belief in Them) Must Exist Because the World Would Be Worse If They Did Not

The consequentialist argument posits that free will and moral responsibility must exist because of the consequences for human society if they did not. This argument comes in two forms. The first is that free will and moral responsibility must exist because the world would be worse off if they did not. The second is that we should *believe* in free will and moral responsibility (whether or not they exist) because the world would be worse off if we did not hold these *beliefs*.

This tracks the way some approach the question of the existence of a god. Some argue that a god must exist because the world would be worse off if a god did not exist, while others argue that a *belief* in a god is desirable (whether or not a god exists) because without that *belief* the world would be worse off.

Of course, one's opinion on whether the world would be better or worse off without a god or free will has no bearing on whether either of them exist. The world might be better off if malaria-carrying mosquitos did not exist, but they still do, at least for now.

The more serious arguments are those that focus on belief. These arguments posit that the world will be better off if people believe in free will and moral responsibility. We should believe in these things even if they are not true or do not make sense.

The Parade of Horribles

Some philosophers have argued that a world without free will and moral responsibility would be so awful that both free will and moral responsibility—or at least a belief in them—must exist. Such philosophers often like to trot out stories that illustrate how horrible a deterministic world would be. The philosopher Daniel Dennett has catalogued a number of these stories. They include those of the Invisible Jailor, the Nefarious Neurosurgeon, the Hideous Hypnotist, the Peremptory Puppeteer, the Cosmic Child Whose Dolls We Are, the Malevolent Mindreader, and the Digger Wasp.[24]

For example, if determinism is true, are we not, in effect, like prisoners in an invisible jail, under the control of an invisible jailor? We think we have freedom, but we do not. The jailor is secretly constraining us. Alternatively, perhaps we are in the clutches of a nefarious neurosurgeon who has secretly implanted electrodes in our brains and uses electrical impulses to control our wants and desires. We act according to those wants and desires, and thus believe we are free. However, to control our actions, all the nefarious neurosurgeon has to do is to stimulate our brains to change our wants and desires. Or maybe we have been hypnotized and our actions are controlled by a hypnotist. Again, we believe we are free, but in reality, the hypnotist controls us. (The Peremptory Puppeteer, the Cosmic Child Whose Dolls We Are, and the Malevolent Mindreader are similar stories.)

The Digger Wasp story is slightly different. The digger wasp is an actual insect with known behaviors. Scientists have learned to manipulate some of these behaviors. If we put the wasp in a particular situation, it will act in a particular way. If we do it repeatedly, the wasp will perform identically. The behavior is completely mechanical, predictable, and determined. We humans could not possibly be like that!

Another example of this type of argument appeared recently in *Brainwashed,* an otherwise fascinating book on the limits of neuroscience. The authors of *Brainwashed* would like you to believe that a world without moral responsibility would be unpleasant. They point to several psychological studies that show the adverse effects. They make several claims. For example,

> In the absence of retribution "victims feel unavenged and therefore devalued and dishonored."[25]

> Society loses faith in the justice system if crimes go unavenged.

They conclude, "a blameless world would be a very chilly place, inhospitable to the warming sentiments of forgiveness, redemption, and gratitude."[26]

In another example, Strawson (1962) argues that because moral responsibility is so important to interpersonal reactions, moral responsibility is justified whether or not the universe is deterministic.[27]

Another consequentialist school of thought carries the appropriate title of *Illusionism* and is associated with Saul Smilansky.[28] Smilansky is a compatibilist. Nevertheless, he argues that, even though *libertarian* free will does not exist, the libertarian view is the easiest to defend. Presumably, the unwashed masses cannot understand compatibilist defenses so we should deceive ourselves (and others) into believing that libertarian free will exists. (Perhaps illusionists fail to consider that the reason that the unwashed masses cannot understand compatibilist defenses is that such defenses do not make sense.)

Another related justification is the belief that people will never abandon the belief in free will so we should just stop worrying about whether it exists. If it exists in the minds of people, then for all intents and purposes, it exists.[29]

The Counterarguments

Again, such approaches proffer reasons why we should believe in free will and accept the idea of moral responsibility. There are several problems with this. The first is that it does violence to the truth. There is no evidence that free will exists and considerable evidence against it. And moral responsibility in the absence of free will is an indefensible notion. To the extent that we value truth, such willful belief in the face of contrary evidence is very problematic.

The second problem is that the truth will eventually come out whether we want it to or not. It is difficult to sustain a belief in something that one rationally knows to be false. The evidence eventually piles up.

In an interesting experimental study, Kim and Hinds discovered that people are more likely to assign blame to robots if the robots are more autonomous and if their decision-making is less transparent.[30] But this means that that the complement must also be true: as people come to understand the deterministic nature of the universe, they will tend to abandon notions of blame and moral responsibility for past actions.

Finally, a world without retribution would not be a chilly place. Some human reactions—including retribution, righteous anger, guilt, regret, and remorse—would become less common. In such a world, we would act much more humanely toward our fellow humans and toward ourselves. Moreover, other human reactions will remain—including happiness, sadness, gratitude, a sense of connection and love.[31] I will say more about this in Part III.

To conclude, if the absence of the belief in the myth of free will and moral responsibility has negative consequences, then so be it. Such is the cost of truth. However, the second point, to which most of this book is devoted, is that accepting the absence of free will and moral responsibility will make the world a better place.

Getting Rid of the Excess Baggage

I am advocating that we accept that the universe is causally or stochastically deterministic and therefore accept that there is no free will and no moral responsibility for our past actions. This is the essence of *afreeism*. (Others have labeled this position *hard determinism* or *hard incompatibilism*, although there are subtle differences implied by these labels.)

In the following exercise, I want you to imagine an intellectual and philosophical trip from libertarianism, through compatibilism, through semicompatibilism, to afreeism.

Imagine first that you are a libertarian. You believe in free will and you do not believe that the universe is stochastically or causally determined. Some things, of course, may be determined, but humans have somehow managed to transcend the laws of physics and can take actions that are neither caused nor random.

In this model, free will implies moral responsibility. People are responsible for actions they take of their own free will and, as a matter of social policy, we are justified in punishing them if they violate social norms. We base our rewards and punishments on the notion that people are morally responsible and deserve blame and punishment for actions that violate moral rules. (Many libertarians also accept other justifications, such as deterrence.) We can diagram the path from free will to a system of rewards and punishment as follows:

Libertarianism

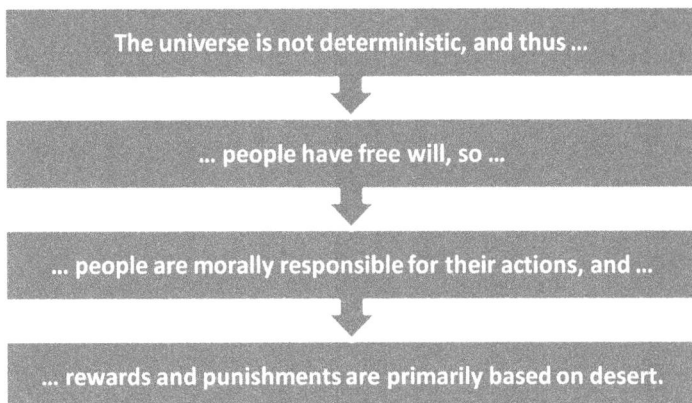

The universe is not deterministic, and thus ...

↓

... people have free will, so ...

↓

... people are morally responsible for their actions, and ...

↓

... rewards and punishments are primarily based on desert.

Frankly, this is how most people think. Because people have free will, we feel justified in rewarding and punishing them based on what they deserve.

However, suppose that by looking at the evidence, you conclude that the world is deterministic. Still, you are not willing to give up the ideas of free will and moral responsibility. You redefine free will as something compatible with the universe being determined. For example, you define free will as simply being able to do what you want, even if your wants have been determined. You have become a compatibilist. Once you have decided that free will exists, you conclude that so does moral responsibility. Again, rewards and punishments are based primarily on the notion that people deserve them. (And, again, compatibilists may accept other rationales as well.) We can diagram the path from free will to our system of rewards and punishment as follows:

Compatibilism

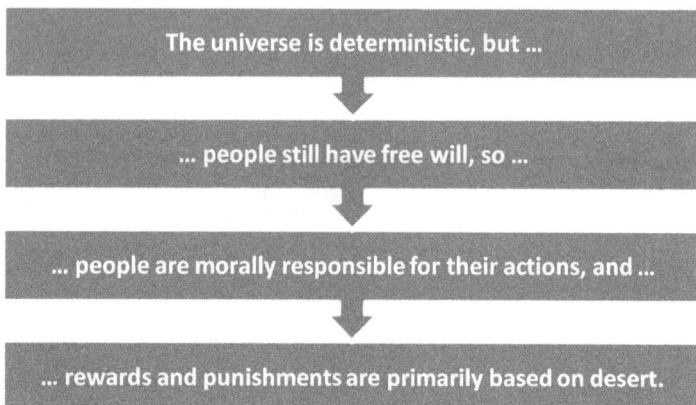

The universe is deterministic, but ...

↓

... people still have free will, so ...

↓

... people are morally responsible for their actions, and ...

↓

... rewards and punishments are primarily based on desert.

Now suppose that you have become uncomfortable with the compatibilist strategy of redefining free will so that it fits with determinism. You decide that it does not make sense to say that a person has free will if that person's actions were determined by a chain of causation beginning with the start of time. You abandon the idea that people have free will. However, you do not want to give up on moral responsibility, so you become a semicompatibilist. The semicompatibilist does not try to defend the notion of free will but instead claims that someone can be morally responsible for an action even if acting without free will. Once we have moral responsibility we can again base our rewards and punishments on the notion that people deserve them for actions that violate moral rules. We can diagram this as follows:

The Counterarguments

Semicompatibilism

The universe Is deterministic, but ...

... people are still morally responsible for their actions, and ...

... rewards and punishments are primarily based on desert.

The semicompatibilist strategy strips away the baggage of needing to prove the existence of free will in a deterministic universe. With that baggage stripped away, the semicompatibilist can make arguments for moral responsibility.

Note that the advantage of stripping away the need to address the notion of free will is not lost on all compatibilists. Daniel Dennett, whose treatise *Elbow Room* is perhaps the most forceful exposition of the compatibilist view, writes in the preface of his newest edition:

> In unpublished lectures I have tentatively explored abandoning the term "free will" altogether—on the grounds that it simply has too many unfortunate and apparently irresistible connotations to survive reform—while persisting with the topic: the conditions underlying the moral responsibility of normal adult human beings.[32]

In other words, Dennett has considered jumping ship from compatibilism to semicompatibilism. (He has not done so yet, at least not in his writings.)

Finally, suppose you take the final step. You conclude that it simply is not right to put moral blame on someone when her actions are completely determined by a causal chain that began long before she was born. You become an afreeist. Nevertheless, you do realize that for society to function you will need a system of rewards and punishments. Likely, this system will be based on things like education, rehabilitation, deterrence, and perhaps occasionally incapacitation. (Of course, these will not be easy issues. For one, we will need to justify punishing someone who lacks free will and moral responsibility.) We can diagram the afreeist view simply as:

Afreeism

The universe is deterministic, so ...

... rewards and punishments are not based on desert but rather on incentives and other consideratons.

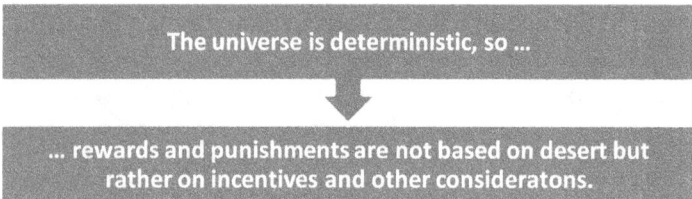

Afreeism strips away all of the baggage of free will and moral responsibility. One can then go directly to the matter of designing a social system that provides rewards and punishments in a way that promotes human flourishing.

Why These Distinctions Matter

One might say that the differences between compatibilists, semicompatibilists, and afreeists are simply a matter of semantics, of definition. All three are determinists, after all, and their differences stem just from competing definitions of free will and moral responsibility. Why does it matter whether we impose a penalty on someone because she committed an act of her own free will, because we believe that she has moral responsibility even in the absence of free will, or because doing so will reform her and deter her or others in the future? Are these just three ways of saying the same thing? Are the philosophical arguments just angels dancing on the head of a pin?

The problem is that when we accept the notion of free will and moral responsibility, we tend to forget that the world is deterministic (even if we intellectually know that it is), and we forget that the criminal who we just convicted had to be there, had to do what she did. Free will and moral responsibility are, in a sense, a shorthand that allows us to make easy decisions (at least, easier decisions) without looking closely at what is to be gained and what is to be lost in punishing an individual. Rather than seeing the individual as someone pushed inexorably by causal forces into what we see before us, we see her as morally suspect, as lacking in humanity, as ultimately something other than us. It is no surprise that empirical studies show that those who are nudged towards a deterministic world-view are less punitive and less vindictive.[33]

And the same applies when we look at ourselves and what we have done. When we buy into free will and moral responsibility, we forget that the world is deterministic, even if we have previously concluded that it is. We get down on ourselves. We see ourselves as blameworthy or guilty and our actions as shameful. We fill ourselves with remorse. Or, conversely, we become full of ourselves.

Libertarians, compatibilists, and semicompatibilists all look at the world similarly. They all believe in desert and retribution. In short, they are all in bed together fighting for the (philosophical) covers. The afreeist has realized that the covers are not enough for any one of these philosophies. The afreeist has gotten out of bed and is throwing wood on the fire. But is it the warming fire in the hearth or a fire that is burning the house down? In a sense, it is both. The house of free will is in flames. Yet, as we shall see, the result is more comfortable than you might imagine.

So, I encourage you to ignore the siren calls of compatibilism and semicompatibilism. Free will does not exist. Neither does moral responsibility for past actions. Trying to define them into existence does more harm than good.

Moving On

By leaving behind the burning house of free will and moral responsibility, we are free to travel lightly and get to the questions that matter to us, and to approach them head-on. These questions include:

1. What social policies should we adopt? What system of rewards and punishments makes the most sense for giving the members of society the best chance to survive and thrive? How should we best distribute the resources of society?

2. How should we deal with other people in our personal lives?

3. How should we deal with ourselves? How can we live productive, satisfying, joyful lives?

We explore these issues in Parts II and III of this book. Before doing so, however, it is useful to note that the roots of afreeism go back thousands of years. The next chapter takes a brief look at this history.

Appendix

The Frankfurt Counterexample
(and Why It Is Wrong)

Compatibilists accept the idea that the world is, or at least may be, deterministic. Nevertheless, they believe in the existence of free will. As you might imagine, it is a tricky maneuver to preserve free will in a deterministic world. Unlike libertarians who effectively reject the laws of physics, chemistry, and neurobiology, compatibilists accept the science and evidence of these disciplines. Their attempts to prove the existence of free will in light of this are interesting, even fascinating. The following is one such attempt.

The Frankfurt Counterexample

The philosopher Harry Frankfurt (1969) created the following thought experiment. (I am following the description of Derk Pereboom.[34]) Afreeists argue that, for a given decision, the inability to do otherwise implies that there was no free will as to that decision.

Afreeists go on to argue that there is never an ability to do otherwise. Frankfurt sought to attack this argument by showing that a decision could be the product of free will even if there is no ability to do otherwise. His argument goes like this:

a. Suppose that philosophical libertarianism is true. That is, assume that humans can make decisions that are neither caused nor random and, as a result, some decisions are the product of free will.

b. Now consider an individual, Mary, who under our libertarian assumption, can make choices of her own free will. She has to decide whether to murder her coworker Jane. The decision is made at time s, shortly before she takes the action, at time t.

c. Suppose we plant an electrode in Mary's brain that can control her behavior in the following way. If Mary does not decide at time s to kill Jane at time t, then the electrode is automatically triggered and causes Mary to decide to kill Jane at time t.

d. Mary decides at time s to kill Jane at time t and does so. The electrode is never triggered.

Frankfurt would have us conclude that Mary killed Jane of her own free will even though she could not have done otherwise. This is supposed to convince us that we can have free will even if we cannot do otherwise. Mary had free will but could not have done otherwise (because of the electrode).

Why The Frankfurt Counterexample Is Wrong

There are two things to say about this. One is that, in a libertarian universe, Mary could have done otherwise. This decision itself is an act of free will in the libertarian view, regardless of what it does or does not lead to. That is, at point s, she could have decided not to kill Jane. If we can observe the electrode, we can even tell which choice she made at that point. If she had decided not to kill Jane then the electrode would have been triggered and we would know about her decision at point s. True, the outcome (killing Jane) would have been the same, in either case. But this is not troubling to the libertarian. Imagine someone coming to a fork in the road. The libertarian would say that the person has the free will to choose either the left road or the right road. To the libertarian, the choice represents free will even if the roads join up again a short distance later and the decision results in the same outcome. Because, under this libertarian assumption, Mary could have done otherwise—deciding not to kill Jane—this exercise does not test whether the ability to do otherwise is consistent with free will.

Another thing to note is that this exercise is carried out in a world where it is already assumed that free will exists. So what it claims is that, in a world where libertarian free will exists, we can find cases where free will exists even though there is no ability to do otherwise. This says nothing about a world in which libertarian free will does not exist.

Of course, a determinist would conclude that Mary, at time s, could not have done other than what she did. Mary had no free will.

Chapter 7

The Origins of Afreeism

AFREEISM HAS DEEP ROOTS. The first foundations for afreeism were laid four thousand years ago when thinkers began to conclude that the universe was governed by universal rules. Stent (2002) reports:

> By the eighteenth century BCE the Sumerians had developed the idea that Marduk—patron god of Babylon—had ordained explicit natural laws whose obeisance by nature generated cosmic order out of cosmic chaos.[35]

In the Sumerian conception, these natural laws come from a god. The next step in this evolution of ideas occurs when the gods themselves become subject to the laws of nature.

Two pre-Socratic philosophers, Leucippus and Democritus, exemplify this approach. About Leucippus, we know almost nothing. (Some scholars even doubt his existence.) What we know about the ideas of Leucippus comes from his student Democritus and even these come to us indirectly, given that only fragments of the writings of Democritus (which were said to be extensive) survive.

Rather we must look to the descriptions of his ideas given by philosophers who were contemporaries (or near-contemporaries) of his.

Leucippus and Democritus are best known for their atomic theory of matter. In essence, they wanted to replace explanations of the world based on the gods with one based on causation. All things in their system are composed of atoms. Atoms had different properties (that is, there were different types of atoms) and these properties determined the properties of the substances that were made up of these atoms. Laws, not the gods, governed the interaction among atoms. Leucippus is reported to have stated,

> Nothing happens in vain, but everything from reason and by necessity.[36]

This is perhaps the earliest known expression of *causal determinism* in western thought. Leucippus and Democritus were not trying explicitly to present an argument against free will. Rather, they wanted to remove the role of the gods in the unfolding of events. Nevertheless, by expounding a model of determinism, they put free will into question.

Plato (Socrates) and Aristotle

Plato, who expressed most of his ideas through the Socratic dialogues, did not directly discuss the problem of free will in a deterministic universe. Indeed, he did not discuss determinism at all. Plato did, however, have a conception of freedom. For Plato freedom involved self-control. Someone who exercises self-control over her emotions and her base instincts is exercising freedom. Someone who is a slave to her passions is not free.[37] Those who are governed by reason are free. Note that under Plato's conception of freedom, if a decision is made through reason, it is free, even if the decision is completely determined. In other words, Plato has chosen a definition of freedom that is compatible with a deterministic universe. This notion that decisions can be simultaneously free and determined has been picked up by modern-day compatibilists.

Aristotle (384BCE–322BCE) made several contributions to the ideas of determinism and free will. First, Aristotle did not believe that all events were caused. He posited the idea of random events. Therefore, Aristotle provided a building block for stochastic determinism. Nevertheless, Aristotle believed in free will and moral responsibility. He suggested that events are 1) caused, 2) random, or 3) up to us. This *tertium quid (third thing)* comprises events that are of our own free will and which in turn result in moral responsibility. It is unclear, however, whether Aristotle was a compatibilist or a libertarian. That is, Aristotle could be saying that certain things are up to us even if they are caused or random. He may be saying that the things that are "up to us" are those actions that are the result of our moral character, even if our moral character is determined. That would make Aristotle a compatibilist because he just redefines free will in a way that does not conflict with determinism. Many modern-day compatibilists see Aristotle in this light.[38]

Another reading of Aristotle, however, is that he believes that the things that are up to us are neither caused nor random but rather come from within. This would make Aristotle a libertarian. Which view Aristotle supported is unimportant to the arguments today so we can leave this debate to the historians of philosophy.

Epicureanism and Stoicism

The Greek philosopher Epicurus (341BCE–270BCE) founded a school of thought now named after him, Epicureanism. Epicureanism is best known for teaching that the pursuit of pleasure is the greatest good. Epicurus adopted Democritus's atomic theory of matter, Democritus's atheism, and Democritus's determinism. However, similar to Aristotle, Epicurus modified Democritus's determinism by adding the idea of randomness (stochastic determinism) to Democritus's atomic theory of matter. He postulated that in the movement of atoms, some atoms could "swerve" randomly. Thus, he rejected the notion of causal determinism in favor of stochastic determinism. Epicurus seemed to understand that causal determinism was a threat to free will and moral responsibility. By rejecting causal determinism in favor of stochastic determinism, Epicurus sought to remove one impediment to free will and seemed also to suggest that these swerves opened up the possibility of moral responsibility. Yet, Epicurus ultimately realized that stochastic determinism does not lead to moral responsibility any more than causal determinism does. Ultimately, Epicurus adopts Aristotle's view that there must be a third way:

> ... some things happen of necessity, others by chance, others through our own agency. ... necessity destroys responsibility and ... chance or fortune is inconstant; whereas our own actions are free, and it is to them that praise and blame naturally attach.[39]

Lucretius (99–55 BCE), a Roman follower of Epicurus, believed that randomness enabled free will although we have no explanation from him on how it might do so.

Stoicism was another school of thought that embraced determinism. Zeno of Citium (c. 336–262 BCE), the founder of Stoicism, postulated a strictly deterministic universe. According to Zeno,

> It is impossible that the cause be present yet that of which it is the cause not obtain.[40]

The Stoic leader Chrysippus (279–approx. 206 BCE) adopted Zeno's view that events are caused but also stated that this is not incompatible with moral responsibility. A person is morally responsible, he claimed, if the cause of his or her action is internal to him or her. That is, if there are no compelling external forces at the time of the decision causing someone to act in a specific way, and when the act is determined by internal desires and reasoning, then the person can be held to be morally responsible. This holds even if the internal desires and reasoning had been determined by a prior chain of causation. In our terminology, Chrysippus was a semicompatibilist.

The Roman Stoic Cicero (106–43 BCE) was also a thoroughgoing determinist:

> By fate, I mean what the Greeks call heimarmen an ordering and sequence of causes, since it is the connection of cause to cause which out of itself produces anything. Consequently nothing has happened which was not going to be, and likewise nothing is going to be of which nature does not contain causes working to bring that very thing about. This makes it intelligible that fate should be, not the fate of superstition, but that of physics, an everlasting cause of things, why past things happened, why present things are now happening, and why future things will be.[41]

To summarize, a number of the philosophers of antiquity realized the deterministic nature of the universe. Some postulated that the universe was causally deterministic while others postulated that the universe was stochastically deter-ministic. They thus laid the foundations for afreeism. None (that we know of), however, were willing to take the next logical step, that of discarding the notions of free will and moral responsibility. This will be left to later philosophers.

Christian Thought

After the fall of Rome and the beginning of the Middle Ages, much of the philosophizing in the west on free will fell to Christian and Jewish theologians. Christian theologians had two problems with their conception of God. One was that God was supposedly both omnipotent and benevolent. If so, why did he permit evil to happen? This problem predates the Christians. Epicurus wrote:

> The gods can either take away evil from the world and will not, or, being willing to do so, cannot; or they neither can nor will, or lastly they are both able and willing. If they have the will to remove evil and cannot, then they are not omnipotent. If they can, but will not, then they are not benevolent. If they are neither able nor willing, then they are neither omnipotent nor benevolent. Lastly, if they are both willing and able to annihilate evil, how does it exist?[42]

Free will solved this problem. Humans could choose good over evil of their own free will. Evil existed only if a person chose evil. Augustine defended this view. He argued that free will is necessary for good since humans could not do good without free will. Unfortunately, because of the fallibility of humans, free will also results in evil. Thus, to have good, we must accept that there will be evil. (The idea that evil is necessary for good will be taken up later by Leibniz.)

Unfortunately, the Christian view of their god had another problem: the omniscience of God. Omniscience implies determinism. If God knows in advance everything that is going to happen, including knowing every choice a human will make in the future, then everything must be determined. Augustine seemed to realize that divine foreknowledge was equivalent to determinism. He wrote:

> This is the predestination of the saints, nothing else: plainly the foreknowledge and preparation of God's benefits, by means of which whoever is to be liberated is most certainly liberated.[43]

In other words, those who would be saved were saved. (And those who would be damned, were damned.) Augustine resolved this conflict in the way that modern compatibilists do. He redefined free will. Free will was acting according to one's desires, even if those desires were completely determined, as they must be because God also knows all past, present, and future desires. By defining free will in this way, divine foreknowledge does not conflict with free will.

This was not the only Christian view of the time. Pelagius, for example, did not believe in predestination. Rather, humans (with the help of God), could freely choose to be saved. How this could be reconciled with divine foreknowledge is not clear. Augustine forcefully attacked this view and it was eventually condemned by the church.

Thomas Aquinas's views on free will are similar to those of Augustine. That is, he accepted both divine foreknowledge and free will and argued that they were not inconsistent. Free will consists of using our rationality to make decisions, guided by moral values. This, he believes, is consistent with God knowing exactly what we will choose.

He does not explain how, given God's complete knowledge of what a person will do, a person can do otherwise.

Jewish Thought

In Judaism, free will was and is a central tenet:

> Free will is granted to all men. If one desires to turn himself to the path of good and be righteous, the choice is his. Should he desire to turn to the path of evil and be wicked, the choice is his.[44]

Nevertheless, by the time of the first century AD there were a variety of views:

> In his treatise, The Antiquities of the Jews, Josephus noted that the three sects differ in their opinions regarding the causation of human actions. The Essenes affirmed that fate determines all actions, and that nothing befalls mankind but what is determined by fate. They therefore rejected the role of free will in the causation of human actions and accepted the view that became known as 'determinism.'

> The Sadducees held that fate plays no role in human affairs, there being no such thing as fate in the first place. They supposed that all our actions are within our control, so that our own righteousness is the cause of our doing what is good and that we are driven by our own folly to doing what is evil. Hence Sadducees believed in free will.

> Finally, the Pharisees ascribed the cause of all human actions to fate. Yet they allowed that acting according to what is right or what is wrong is mainly within our own power, even though fate plays some causative role in every action. The Pharisees' argument regarding the compatibility of fate (and God's foreknowledge of it) with the

exercise of human free will was adopted some 300 years later by St. Augustine.[45]

Later Jewish scholars recognized the conflict between free will and divine foreknowledge. Maimonides, who was born c. 1135 CE, was well aware of the problem but argued that free will was compatible with divine foreknowledge. The error in thinking otherwise was equating knowledge of God with knowledge of humans. Just as God has a different existence than humans, God's knowledge is somehow different than human knowledge. If a person were to know with complete accuracy that something will happen, this would foreclose the possibility of anything else happening. Thus, there is no free will. However, this is not true of God's knowledge. God's knowing that something will happen does not foreclose the possibility of something else happening, even though something else will not happen.[46] Instead of redefining free will, this odd gambit recasts the meaning of knowledge, rendering it virtually unrecognizable.

Other Jewish writers did not accept this explanation. Gersonides (Levi ben Gershon) (1288-1344) concluded that free will precludes God's knowing that something will definitively happen. Rather, God's perfect knowledge extends to knowing the possibilities of events subject to human will, but not to the outcomes:[47]

> To affirm that God knows the possible only as possible is not detracting from His supreme intelligence, for to know things as they are means to know them well (Milḥamot, iii. 106).[48]

Ḥasdai Crescas (1340-1410), on the other hand, accepted determinism and the idea that, when considered in the context of the universe, humans cannot do other than what causation dictates. Yet, the Torah speaks of free will and therefore there must be some conception of free will that is compatible with determinism. The Jewish Encyclopedia describes Crescas's view thusly:

> Crescas, therefore, concludes that human will is free in certain respects, but limited in others. Will acts as a free agent when considered alone, but operates by necessity when regarded in relation to the remote cause; or will operates in freedom, both per se and with regard to the provoking cause, but it is bound if analyzed with reference to the divine omniscience. Man feels himself free; therefore he is responsible, and must be rewarded or punished.[49]

In short, most Christian and Jewish thinkers needed the idea of free will to solve the problem of evil. Yet, they also had to confront the idea that free will is inconsistent with divine omniscience. With free will, one can explain evil but not omniscience. Without free will, one can explain omniscience but not evil. This tension has never been resolved.

Buddhism, Confucianism, and Taoism

Because Buddhism, Confucianism, and Taoism have no conception of a deity, they did not have to confront the problem of how evil could exist with an all-powerful and all-good god. They therefore did not have to resort to free will as the solution to this problem. As a result, free will is not a central tenet of any of these schools of thought. So perhaps we can learn something about behavior in a world without free will by examining these traditions.

Buddhism was founded by Siddhartha Gautama. There is dispute over when he lived: some scholars date his birth as early as the 560s BCE and others date his birth about a century later. Confucius was probably born around 550

BCE. Lao Tzu, the purported founder of Taoism, may have been born anywhere from the sixth century to the fourth century BCE, although some scholars doubt he existed at all. Again, none of these three belief systems hypothesize the existence of a god. Buddha, for example, rejected the idea of a god, because he believed it was inconsistent with the existence of evil and suffering.[50] Rather these belief systems consisted of methods and ideas about how to live. Buddhism focused on suffering and how to live with it and how to mitigate it. This was approached through the Eight-Fold Path. Confucianism and Taoism referred to their paths as the Tao ("The Path"), although with different emphases:

> The main difference between the Tao of Confucianism and the Tao of Taoism is that Confucianism stresses the Tao of non-natural human society while Taoism stresses the Tao of natural phenomena. Thus the humanistic Sacred Way of Confucianism, being concerned with the political order and the practical life of the person, tries to deal with the problems inherent in social relationships. It prescribes social norms and moral precepts, for which the ways of nature are of little relevance. The natural Sacred Way of Taoism, by contrast, is a transcendental moral philosophy, whose main relevance is for the person's inner life rather than for her social relations.[51]

Although Buddhism does not address the issue of free will, its writings do evidence a causal worldview that is so thoroughgoing that it eschews boundaries, conceiving of the universe as a vast seamless causal web. Buddhism's denial of self rejects the frontier between persons and the rest of the universe. Because its moral prescriptions flow from this worldview, Buddhism rejects anger and retribution as valid reactions. Meditation is one means of overcoming these emotions.[52]

Although its emphasis differs from that of Buddhism, Confucianism also rejects both free will and retribution as a justification for punishment.

> ... Confucius did not view the moral life as freely willed choices.... These problems do not exist for Confucius because he does not believe that moral decisions involve any choice in the first place. Classical Western morality embedded in the Greco-Judeo-Christian tradition regards punishment as a retributive response to past moral wrong-doing.... This was not Confucius' view of the function of punishment, because he lacked the concept of morally responsible agents. He shared the view generally prevalent in Ancient China (and among the strain of Western moral philosophers inspired by Aristotle), that punishment serves as a utilitarian deterrent for the commission of future crimes, rather than as a just retribution to erase guilt for past crimes.... According to the Confucian view, the proper response to a failure to conform to the prescribed ritual order ... is not guilt for having made a blameworthy autonomous choice, but self-education to remedy a deficiency in one's moral development.[53]

Because Confucianism provides a rationale for punishment that is independent of free will and moral responsibility, it addresses a key concern of afreeism. How can we punish in the absence of moral responsibility? We examine this in greater depth in Chapter 8.

Finally, Taoism also conceives of nature as a system of which humans are a part. Taoism asserts that we have a will but is silent as to whether that will is free.

Renaissance, Enlightenment and Beyond

During the Renaissance and the Enlightenment, the issue of free will passed from the churchmen back to the philosophers. These philosophers were less concerned with the problem of evil and more concerned about how free will could be reconciled with the deterministic universe for which the new science was contributing additional evidence. Thomas Hobbes (1588-1679) was perhaps the first "modern" compatibilist. Hobbes believed that everything was the result of a web of causes—even the choices of humans.

> That which I say necessitates and determinates every action is the sum of all those things which, being now existent, conduce and concur to the production of the action hereafter, whereof if any one thing were wanting, the effect could not be produced. This concourse of causes, whereof every one is determined to be such as it is by a like concourse of former causes, may well be called the decree of God.[54]

Hobbes believed that God was the original cause. God set the universe in motion. God is uncaused and possesses free will. Everything else, however, including human actions, is caused.

Because of this determinism, Hobbes did not believe that the will is free, but he did believe that an *act* is free if there are no *external* impediments. However, because all decisions are determined, Hobbes did not believe that a person could ever be blameworthy. He did believe that there were moral obligations and that these moral obligations could cause human action. He also believed that punishment was justified by deterrence. As such, Hobbes was perhaps the first "modern" afreeist.

In contrast, Hobbes's contemporary, the French philosopher René Descartes (1596-1650), is perhaps the first "modern" libertarian. Descartes is also the modern originator of the mind-body problem. (Plato had a version of this in his conception of this dualism.[55]) That is, Descartes divided reality into body (the physical world) and mind (thoughts). While the physical world is deterministic, free will exists in the mind. Moreover, he believed that the mind could affect the physical world.

> Descartes ... believed that if the freedom of the human being is to be preserved, the soul must be exempt from the kind of deterministic laws that rule over the material universe.[56]

Accordingly, Descartes held that thoughts were somehow exempt from the laws of physics and were not part of the physical world. Because of this, humans can choose between good and evil and are morally responsible.

Baruch Spinoza (1632-1677) was a thoroughgoing determinist. Although he couched his determinism in theism, Spinoza's God was, in effect, nature. Human action is completely determined, even though it may not seem so to humans.

> Nothing in the universe is contingent, but all things are conditioned to exist and operate in a particular manner by the necessity of the divine nature.[57]

> ... all things ... flow from the same necessity; in the same way as from the nature of a triangle it follows from eternity and for eternity, that its three interior angles are equal to two right angles.[58]

> ... men think themselves free inasmuch as they are conscious of their volitions and desires, and never even

114

dream, in their ignorance, of the causes which have disposed them so to wish and desire.[59]

Spinoza did not believe in free will, but he did believe in a deterministic sort of freedom. Freedom was being free of one's passions and acting true to one's nature. (This is very Platonic.) This is accomplished through replacing a desire for things (which we cannot control) with a desire for the knowledge and understanding of God, that is, of nature. Because of his determinism, Spinoza did not believe in many of the virtues of his day. To Spinoza, virtues are those qualities that flow from reason. Vices flow from the passions. Guilt, repentance, pity, etc., flow from the passions and thus are not virtues. Freeing oneself of these destructive impulses is possible if one understands the deterministic nature of the universe. At the end of Part II of *The Ethics,* he states that his deterministic philosophy enjoins us "to hate no one, to disesteem no one, to mock no one, to be angry at no one, to envy no one."

Spinoza's philosophy leads him to argue for religious tolerance and freedom of speech.[60] Furthermore, because the universe is causal, and because we are ourselves causes, if we want to effect change, we should increase our understanding of this universe.

Spinoza's ideas were so radical for his day that he was excommunicated from his Jewish community in Amsterdam. (The excommunication probably had more to do with the community not wanting to have the Dutch authorities come down on it. Spinoza's Jewish community comprised Portuguese refugees from the Spanish/Portuguese Inquisition and so probably felt vulnerable in Protestant Netherlands, even though the authorities in the Netherlands were relatively tolerant for their day.)

Spinoza's determinism and ethics come very close to the afreeism that this book advocates and we will discuss some of these ideas in later chapters.

In the meantime, other philosophers continued to argue for the existence of free will. An example is Gottfried Wilhelm Leibniz (1646-1716). Leibniz was a compatibilist in that he believed that free will was compatible with God's ability to know everything that will happen in the future. Because God knows how everything will unfold, humans cannot do anything that contradicts this knowledge. Thus, everything is determined. Nevertheless, humans do deliberate and, on the basis of this deliberation, make decisions. They therefore have sufficient free will for moral responsibility.

On the question of evil, Leibniz takes a slightly different approach than that of the Christian and Jewish theologians discussed above. Leibniz believed that God did not necessarily desire evil but that evil was necessary for harmony. In other words, even God was constrained by nature. He had to choose to create a world among various possible worlds. Famously, Leibniz postulated that, given these constraints and the goodness of God, God created the "best of all possible worlds." Given his view on evil, Leibniz did not require the concept of free will to solve the problem of evil. Nevertheless, Leibniz did believe in a compatibilist form of free will and moral responsibility.

Among the British empiricists, John Locke (1632-1704) did not directly confront the issue as to whether the will could be free in a deterministic universe. Locke's conception of freedom is the ability to do what the will dictates:

> Freedom of action, on Locke's account, is a matter of being able to do what one wills and being able to forbear what one wills to forbear. . . . [T]he mere fact (if it is a fact) that our actions are determined by the laws of nature and

antecedent events does not threaten our freedom with respect to their performance. As Locke makes clear, if the door to my room is unlocked, I am free with respect to the act of leaving the room, because I have the ability to stay or leave as I will. It is only when the door is locked, or when I am chained, or when my path is blocked, or something else deprives me of the ability to stay or leave, that I am unfree with respect to the act of leaving.[61]

Although Locke does not discuss the tension between free will and determinism directly, he does provide the foundation for the compatibilist theories of Hume and later philosophers.

Bishop George Berkeley (1685-1753) was a libertarian who believed that will originated nondeterministically within persons. The decisions of a person, while influenced by the environment and subject to reasoning, were not deterministically caused. Berkeley never explains why humans are somehow exempt from the laws of nature.

David Hume (1711-1776) believed that all actions were caused. Nevertheless, he adopted the compatibilist strategy of defining an act as free if it was caused by the desires of the actor. That is, even though the actor could not do otherwise (because causal factors determined the actor's desires), there is nevertheless free will and moral responsibility. Similar to other compatibilists, Hume never explained why actions that had to happen can be the basis of moral responsibility.

Immanuel Kant (1724-1804) dismissed Hume's compatibilist approach to free will, calling it a "wretched subterfuge." Kant believed that true freedom had to be "entirely independent of natural law." To achieve this, Kant created two interacting worlds, the noumenal world and the phenomenal world.

> Dividing the world into one of natural causality [the phenomenal world], ruled by the laws of nature, and a noumenal world governed by freedom and ruled by moral law, Kant solves the problem of free will by restricting it to the noumenal world.[62]

The will exists in the noumenal world, which is not bound by the laws of nature but rather by the laws of morality. Because the will is not bound by the laws of nature, it is free. Because the will is subject to the laws of morality, humans are morally responsible for their actions. Because Kant believed that some human action is not physically caused, we can consider him a libertarian. As with other libertarians, Kant never gave a convincing account as to why human action is exempt from the laws of nature. It is indicative of the power of the illusion of free will that even a brilliant thinker such as Kant could not conceive of a world without it and would turn to almost magical thinking (the creation of a mysterious noumenal world) to justify it.

Against this almost mystical conception of human actions, the Enlightenment was producing a growing belief in science and the causal nature of the universe. Pierre-Simon Laplace (1749-1827) was one of the most insistent advocates of the deterministic universe. Laplace was a mathematician and scientist of great accomplishment. As a mathematician, he is known for the Laplace Transform, the Laplace Equation, and the Laplacian Differential Operator. He provided a basis in calculus for classical mechanics, studied nebulae, and proposed the existence of black holes. He pioneered and promoted the Bayesian approach to probability.

For our purposes, Laplace is known for Laplace's Demon, a description of determinism. He wrote:

We ought then to regard the present state of the universe as the effect of its anterior state and as the cause of the one which is to follow. Given for one instant an intelligence which could comprehend all the forces by which nature is animated and the respective positions of the beings which compose it—an intelligence sufficiently vast to submit these data to analysis—it would embrace in the same formula both the movements of the largest bodies in the universe and those of the lightest atom; for it, nothing would be uncertain and the future, as the past, would be present to its eyes.[63]

The "intelligence" that Laplace refers to has become known as Laplace's Demon. In Laplace's deterministic universe there is no room for free will, as everything unfolds deterministically. (Less known, the scientist Roger Joseph Boscovich presented a nearly identical view 50 years earlier.[64])

Indeed, there is no randomness in Laplace's universe. Consistent with Laplace's Bayesian approach to probability, all apparent randomness comes from a lack of knowledge.

The nineteenth century witnessed additional developments. Inquiries turned to the workings of the mind. Schopenhauer (1788-1860) conceived the will as a subconscious force that derives from the character of the individual. This will is free in the sense that the will determines actions. Yet the will itself, because it is subconscious and because it is determined by the character of the individual, is beyond the conscious control of the individual. Freedom of choice, therefore, is just an illusion. Nevertheless, because the will derives from the character of the individual, moral responsibility exists. By imposing moral responsibility, we can influence the choices that the will makes. (However, Schopenhauer was skeptical as to whether punishment could affect character and the will itself.)

Nietzsche (1844-1900) picked up Schopenhauer's idea that actions follow from an unconscious will. Nietzsche did not follow Schopenhauer's characterization of the will as free. Rather, he used this idea to characterize human actions as a product of strict determinism. (This difference with Schopenhauer may just be semantic since Schopenhauer did not believe that human actions were at all free.) The appeal to the unconscious was Nietzsche's main argument against the freedom of the will. We cannot control our unconscious states (we do not have access to them) and so we cannot control our will. Our will determines our actions. Nietzsche also argued that nothing is the cause of itself, and because freedom of the will would imply something causing itself, it follows that freedom of the will is absurd. Therefore, our actions are not free

Note that this view eliminates compatibilist conceptions of free will. Compatibilists posit that free will is doing what one wants, even if what one wants is causally determined. For Nietzsche, however, one does not consciously do what one wants. The will operates unconsciously.

Afreeism in Historical Context

Musings on causation, determinism, free will, and moral responsibility have continued apace throughout the twentieth century and into the twenty-first century. Academia.com, a portal for research papers lists (at the time of this writing) over 70,000 articles under the rubric "free will and determinism." However, the landscape has not changed much. Some continue to argue that humans are somehow exempt from the laws of nature and causation and are capable of making choices that are neither caused nor random. Others have conceded that the universe is deterministic and that all choices are caused but argue that free will nevertheless exists. They accomplish this by changing the definition of free will. They then claim that this newly-defined free will implies moral responsibility. However, they never adequately explain how someone can be morally responsible for acts that simply had to happen. Finally, some understand that the deterministic nature of the universe means that there is neither free will nor moral responsibility. This is the afreeist understanding.

Again, afreeism is not a new idea. The Greeks of antiquity understood that the universe was causally or stochastically deterministic. The nontheistic traditions of Buddhism and Confucianism discarded the notion of free will and developed moral practices that were independent of it. In the West, several philosophers, such as Thomas Hobbes and Baruch Spinoza, rejected the notion of moral responsibility in favor of alternative rationales for punishment. Because discarding the notion of free will has implications in terms of social policy, in how we treat other people, and in how we view ourselves, we should try to glean everything we can from those who first confronted these issues. We will be returning to some of these ideas in future chapters.

Part II

Afreeist Social Policy

Chapter 8

Principles of Afreeist Social Policy

WE ALL HAVE SOME INFLUENCE over social policy. Some of us are political leaders, others are government bureaucrats, and still others are members of influential groups, such as NGOs, industry lobbies, or civic organizations. A great many of us vote.

On a grand scale, social policy is about organizing society in a way that promotes human flourishing. On a smaller scale, it is about using the levers of government to solve social problems. How do we address crime, the opioid epidemic, economic inequality, educational opportunities, foreign policy, pollution and global warming, immigration, and inflation?

Our philosophical outlook shapes the way we approach government and social policy. Political ideologies run the gamut: liberal, conservative, socialist, libertarian, communist, anarchist, and others. Within these categories are various subcategories, such as traditional conservative, tea party conservative, alt-right conservative, traditional liberal, progressive liberal, etc. Indeed, labels are not likely to capture the nuances of any one person's political philosophy.

Political ideology affects how we approach social problems. For example, conservatives and liberals have quite different views on the effectiveness of markets, the role of governments, the effects of inequality, and even the meaning of freedom.

I am not going to opine on the merits or demerits of anyone's political philosophy. My goal is narrower, but perhaps more fundamental. I want to examine how an understanding that the universe is deterministic might affect what we believe to be the best social policies. How will it change the way we look at social problems and potential solutions?

Three Points of Departure

The universe is deterministic, either causally or stochastically. As a result, a person's actions are determined. As for social policy, this fact leads to at least three implications and three associated areas of inquiry.

First, the fact that the universe is deterministic implies that no person is blameworthy for any actions that she takes. That is, no one *deserves* blame or punishment. This leads to questions about how the criminal law system and other methods of social control, such as shame and guilt, can work.

Second, the fact that the universe is deterministic implies that no one *deserves* praise or rewards for accomplishments. This leads to questions about how we should distribute wealth, income, and other societal benefits.

Finally, the fact that the universe is deterministic creates questions about the meaning of freedom and whether it exists at all.

In the chapters that follow, I address issues involving the criminal law system (Chapter 10); wealth, income, and inequality (Chapter 11); and freedom (Chapter 12). I discuss some additional policy implications in Chapter 13. Before looking at these specific ideas, however, I will give an overview of some of the general principles that will animate those discussions of social policy.

The Myth of Deservedness

Bill Gates Sr.'s Thought Experiment

In Chuck Collin's book, *Born on Third Base*, he describes a talk that Bill Gates Sr. gave to a group of business leaders. (Chuck and Bill were promoting a book arguing in favor of the inheritance tax.) Bill tells a story. God is about to send two new souls to earth, two new potential entrepreneurs. The following are Bill's words:

> [God] summons . . . the next two beings about to be born on Earth [and] explains to these two spirits that one of them will be born in the United States and the other will be born in an impoverished nation in the global south. [God] recognizes that the United States has an advanced infrastructure of public health, stability, education, and market mechanisms that enhance opportunity [and] understands that some humans might consider it a privilege or advantage to be born in such a society. The spirits are instructed to write the percentage of their net worth they pledge to God's treasury on the day they die.

Whoever offers the highest percentage will have the good fortune to be born in the United States.[65]

Bill then asks the assembled business leaders to write down on a piece of paper the amount that they would bid in this situation. He then asks, for a show of hands. How many wrote down 25% or less. Zero. How many wrote down 50%? Zero. How many wrote down 75%? Three. How many wrote down 100%? Everyone else.

Chuck Collins uses this story to combat what he calls the *myth of deservedness*, the idea that a person somehow deserves everything they get because they are smart and worked hard. This is a myth that affects many people, but particularly the very rich. Bill Gates Sr.'s parable helps people realize that accomplishment is the result of many, many causal factors. Intelligence and hard work are just a small part of this. Many other elements, such as one's birthplace, play a significant role.

The Illusion of Accomplishment

Chuck and Bill's story is a step in the right direction. However, it does not go nearly far enough. First, because the universe is deterministic, all actions and outcomes are determined. Even if one's accomplishments were solely the result of intelligence and hard work, the benefits of accomplishment are still not deserved. Both intelligence and the propensity to work hard are completely determined by causes existing before the actor was born. This is not a question of nature versus nurture. Both nature and nurture are determined. So, the actions taken and the success achieved are all completely determined. They simply had to be. It makes no sense to say that someone *deserves* a large income, vast wealth, or even happiness. If we do praise or reward people for supposed accomplishments, it has to be based on some other reason and not on the myth that they deserve it for what they did.

The Illusion of Failure

The other side of the coin is that failure is undeserved as well. One aspect of this is moral failure, which we discussed in Chapter 4 on moral responsibility. Moral failure can cause pain, suffering, and loss. Nevertheless, we concluded that no person deserves blame or punishment based on moral failure because she could not have done otherwise. Put another way, we are all innocents. All of us. All the time.

In short, we cannot justify punishment on the basis that a person *deserves* to be punished. Retribution—the notion that people should get what they deserve—never makes sense because people never deserve anything. This is not to say that we should never punish but rather that punishment must be based on other principles besides deservedness— on principles of deterrence, public health, education, incapacitation, or the like. Furthermore, we must contend with the notion that, no matter what we do, punishment always involves punishing innocents. (After all, everyone is always innocent.) In a deterrence model, for example, we are punishing innocents to deter others. How can this be morally justified? Chapter 10 examines this and other issues of crime and punishment.

Other types of failure are also completely determined. If one fails at business, one does not *deserve* the consequences of that failure. Likewise, one does not *deserve* the consequences of failing health, even if one contributed to it by overeating, refusing to exercise, overusing alcohol or recreational drugs, or engaging in risky activities. All of these actions were determined, as were the consequences. There is no sense in which any of the consequences are deserved. Again, that does not mean that we never permit or impose negative consequences. There may be good reasons to do so. Deservedness, however, is not one of them.

The Equality Principle

The *illusion of accomplishment* and the *illusion of failure* are both manifestations of the *myth of deservedness*. Understanding this has profound consequences for how we view social policy. It is hard to justify in any moral sense why some people die of starvation or live in wretched conditions, while others have wealth that would be enough to feed, clothe, and take care of millions of people.

Since no one deserves anything, should we not try to distribute the benefits of society as equally as possible? Imagine that you are given a million dollars and you are asked to distribute this money among 1000 people about whom you know nothing. How would you do it? Knowing nothing, you would likely distribute it evenly. However, there may be reasons to deviate from strict equality, such as to provide incentives. But deviating based on desert is not justified. This leads to the following Equality Principle:

The Equality Principle

1. Unless there are reasons for doing otherwise, the costs and benefits of society should be distributed equally.

2. Deservedness cannot be a reason for distributing the costs and benefits of society unequally.

The equality principle is probably the most important takeaway from this chapter. We will consider reasons why we might deviate from strict equality in Chapter 11.

Freedom

Another important social issue and societal value is freedom. Wars have been fought in the name of freedom. Songs have been written proclaiming it. We hear about it all the time as politicians rail against government regulation. Freedoms are enshrined in the United States Constitution: freedom of speech, of the press, and of religion.

Yet the universe is deterministic. All of our actions had to happen. Given this, in what sense can we be free? In what sense is freedom a value? Perhaps freedom is an illusion too.

In Chapter 5, I tried to convince you that the world, as seen through the deterministic lens of causation, appears differently looking forward in time and looking backward toward the past. Forward, the world appears full of possibilities, and because of causation, what we do makes a difference. Looking backward, we see that what we did—what anyone did—had to happen.

The issue of freedom is more involved than the issue of autonomy. Freedom includes concepts of positive freedom and negative freedom, of political, economic, and physical freedom. It warrants more discussion. Interestingly, freedom can be an important societal value even in a determinist universe. We simply need to define it correctly. Chapter 12 is devoted to these ideas.

Principles of Social Policy

To recap, afreeism requires us to look at the world the way it is. The world is deterministic; there is no free will. Because of this, deservedness is a myth. This applies both to the positive and to the negative. On the positive side, this means no one deserves praise or rewards. One's accomplishments simply had to happen. We may enjoy the ride, enjoy that we were made instruments of those accomplishments, but we do not *deserve* to be rewarded. Nevertheless, there may be good reasons to reward people.

Likewise, one's failures, even moral failures, had to happen. Someone may be unfortunate enough to have committed a criminal act. Yet the causes of this act predate the actor; the criminal is not to blame. If we do decide to punish criminals, we must base it on something other than deservedness.

Taking the positive and negative together we arrive at the *Equality Principle*: no one *deserves* to be treated better or worse than another. If we choose as a society to treat one person better or worse than another, we need other reasons. Such reasons do exist, but without deservedness, society will look different than it does now. That is what the following chapters are about.

Chapter 9

The Sinvergüenza Problem

WHEN WE TALK ABOUT SOCIAL POLICY, we are confronted with the question of why people do what they do. We have moral rules and we expect people to abide by them. But what causes them to do so, especially since doing so often involves substantial personal costs?

We can divide social control into two (not completely exclusive) categories: internal controls and external controls. Internal controls involve negative feelings like guilt, shame, regret, and remorse, and positive feelings such as feelings of pride, satisfaction, and accomplishment. Internal controls may also involve empathy and compassion. External controls are punishments and rewards that are applied by others. These could include criminal penalties, civil fines, and physical constraints. External controls can be formal and institutional, such as those doled out by the criminal justice system, or informal, such as shaming, shunning, or verbal rebukes.

In this chapter, I look at internal controls. In the following chapter on crime and punishment, I address external controls.

The Problem

So here is the problem. If no one could have done otherwise, then there is no justification for feelings of guilt, remorse, or regret. And without these emotions, what becomes of society?

Suppose, for example, that I am married and thinking about cheating on my wife. I have made all of the calculations for a successful extramarital affair. I have concluded that I can do so safely and that my wife will never find out. I am very sure of this. I do understand that cheating violates the promises that I have made. I would not do it if there were any likelihood of being discovered. But I won't be discovered. Given these assumptions, I can reason as follows. If I cheat, it will bring me pleasure. Furthermore, because I understand that the world is deterministic, I know that if I do cheat it was because of a chain of causation that flows from states of the world that existed before I was even born. I know this, and because I know this, I will not feel any guilt, regret, or remorse when I do cheat. After all, how can I blame myself? Since there is no blame, there are no negative consequences to cheating, just pleasure. So, I cheat. I say that I could not have done otherwise. And I am right about that!

Suppose now, upon further thought, I conclude that it may not be so easy to keep my affair private. I believe that I can do so, but I also realize that the best-laid plans often go awry. It is possible, I believe, that my wife could someday learn about my cheating. If she does, she will be tremendously hurt. It could end up in divorce. The children, too, will be hurt. Despite my desire to have an affair, I love my wife and kids and am worried about the pain I might cause. I am empathetic. Her pain will cause me pain. Still, I anticipate that the pleasure of cheating will be so great that I am willing to take that chance. Because the world is deterministic, I realize that, although I may be in a world of hurt, the one hurt that I will not experience is remorse. How could I be remorseful for something that had to be? So, after weighing all the pros and cons, I cheat.

In both cases above it could be true that—if I were capable of experiencing remorse, regret, or guilt (for example, if I did believe in free will)—my capacity for those emotions would tip the scales in favor of me not cheating. These anticipated feelings, when added to the other negatives of cheating, may result in me not cheating.

What this story says is that the realization that the world is deterministic could remove an important tool for incentivizing good social behavior. Without guilt, shame, regret, or remorse, I am more likely to engage in antisocial behavior. And cheating on my wife is just the tip of the iceberg. What if my marriage is falling apart, what if I have grown to dislike my wife intensely, what if—rather than divorce her—I decide simply to have her killed in order to collect insurance. If I am a determinist, I should not feel remorse for that either.

The Sinvergüenza Problem

A sinvergüenza is a Spanish term for someone incapable of feeling shame and who therefore engages in shameful behavior. (*Sin* means *without* and *vergüenza* means *shame*. The pronunciation is SEEN-bair-GWEN-za.) A common

English translation of sinvergüenza is *scoundrel.* The sinvergüenza problem, then, is the fear of what happens to behavior when we take away shame, guilt, regret, and remorse.

Of course, we should not overstate the problem. Knowledge of the deterministic nature of the universe will not turn someone into a sociopath. In the first example above, I still care about my wife. I do not want her to feel pain. I am empathetic; I treat her pain as if it were my own. I will feel badly for her and for me if I am discovered. All of these feelings affect my behavior, and as a result, I may not cheat on her.

Nevertheless, we should acknowledge that the sinvergüenza problem is something of a concern. Indeed, we might predict empirically that those who realize that the universe is deterministic will engage in more antisocial behavior than those who believe in free will and feel the attendant shame, guilt, remorse, and regret that this entails. Some studies have indicated exactly that. But others have suggested quite the opposite.

Studies on the effects of a deterministic worldview have been undertaken by several researchers. Many of these studies employ experimental subjects and use some variation of the following procedure:

1. Researchers separate the subjects into two groups.

2. Each group reads a passage. For one group, the passage is an explanation about, for example, how neuroscience has concluded that a person's supposed free choice is precisely determined by neurological processes. The other group reads a passage unrelated to determinism.

3. Both groups are given a problem with choices. For example, both groups may be given the opportunity to cheat on a test or to select the punishment for some specified wrongdoer.

4. The choices are recorded by the researcher and analyzed for propensities.

In some of these studies, researchers found that people who have a greater belief in determinism are more likely to exhibit antisocial behavior. For example, they are:

1. less likely to help,[66]

2. more likely to cheat,[67] and

3. more likely to act aggressively.[68]

In other studies, researchers found that people who have a greater belief in determinism are more likely to exhibit prosocial behaviors. For example, they are:

1. less likely to take immoral actions,[69]

2. less likely to be punitive,[70] and

3. less likely to act vindictively.[71]

We should note that the studies involve subjects who have not had time to reflect on determinism and how it should affect their daily lives and actions. In these studies, researchers nudged those in the test group into a deterministic mindset and then immediately asked these subjects to make a decision. Researchers did not ask the control group to change their outlooks at all. If the researchers had given the test groups time to reflect, perhaps the outcomes would have been different.

Nevertheless, one might reasonably worry that the elimination of shame, guilt, remorse, and regret, might remove some of the incentives for good social behavior. We, as afreeists, cannot ignore this. I will address these fears below.

Moral Responsibility and Social Control

The sinvergüenza problem is just another aspect of the larger problem of moral responsibility. In a deterministic world, there is no moral responsibility for actions that have been taken. From a societal standpoint, the question becomes, if the whole world jettisons feelings of guilt, remorse, or regret, why will anyone ever comply with moral rules?

Why Civilization As We Know It Will Not End

The upshot of the above is that we must learn to live in a world where moral responsibility for past actions does not make sense. There is a tendency to believe that such a world would be untenable, that unchecked forces of human nature will drive us to societal destruction. I do not believe that this is the case. Rather, I believe that the world will be better off once we come to our senses and see the world the way it truly is. Here are some things to consider.

We Cannot Put the Genie Back in the Bottle

First, we must acknowledge that we cannot change the fact that the world is deterministic. The supposed baleful effects of determinism come not from the fact that the universe is deterministic, but rather from people *learning* that the universe is deterministic.

So, we are confronted with a conundrum. Should we insist that people believe in free will, even if it does not exist, in order to maintain the social controls provided by feelings of guilt, remorse, regret, and shame? I believe that it is better to confront the truth as it is. Indeed, it may not even be possible to put the genie of afreeism back in the bottle. Once someone becomes convinced of a truth and is surrounded by the evidence of it, it may be hard to convince that person to unlearn that truth. Once we eat from the tree of knowledge, we are stuck with that knowledge even if, as in the Garden of Eden, the effects are catastrophic.

We can analogize this to theism, the belief in a god. If a person loses her faith in a god because she concludes that there is simply no evidence for the proposition and much evidence against it, can we convince her to revert to her original belief simply because doing so might make society better? I am skeptical about our ability as humans to believe on demand. Evidence supports the deterministic worldview and we should deal with it. We cannot simply choose to believe something we know is not true.

However, the Genie May Never Fully Emerge

Nevertheless, there is a good chance that the genie will never fully materialize. The belief in free will is so strongly held by so many people that perhaps there is little danger in afreeism becoming the norm. Even people who are rational thinkers in most aspects of their lives often have blind spots when it comes to things like religion and free will. So maybe those concerned about afreeism becoming a widely shared view, bringing the concomitant negative consequences they envision, can relax.

These fears are misguided for a more important reason, however. Afreeism, properly understood, carries an array of positive social and personal implications that we will forgo if we cling to the myth of free will.

Even if Afreeism is Widely Accepted, Antisocial Behavior Will Be Reined in by Other Forms of Social Control

Even if afreeism becomes the prevailing worldview, it is unlikely that we will see any significant uptick in antisocial behavior because there are so many other mechanisms of social control. Empathy, as mentioned in an example above, works toward promoting prosocial behavior. Empathy, perhaps a social evolutionary adaptation, allows humans to organize and work together. Feeling the pleasure and pain of other people is a powerful check on antisocial behavior.[72]

In addition, humans internalize societal rules through socialization. Humans are social animals. Most people follow rules, especially moral rules, not because of informal or formal penalties, but because they internalize those rules during childhood. These internalized social rules make sense to most of us and, in any case, are second nature to many humans. A famous study by Joshua Greene and Joseph Paxton in which they allowed subjects to cheat (while monitoring their brain activity) found that, for those who did not cheat, resisting the temptation to cheat did not involve any internal conflict. In describing the study Robert Sapolsky reports:

> Resisting temptation is as implicit as walking up stairs, or thinking "Wednesday" after hearing "Monday, Tuesday," or as that first piece of regulation we mastered way back when, being potty trained. . . . [I]t's not a function of what

Kohlbergian stage you're at; it's what moral imperatives have been hammered into you with such urgency and consistency that doing the right thing has virtually become a spinal reflex.[73]

Of course, not every subject in the study resisted the temptation to cheat. And some struggled with the decision. Nevertheless, the study demonstrated the existence of internal social controls that have nothing to do with guilt, regret, or remorse.

Finally, sometimes there are actual external incentives, like fines and jail time, which rein in antisocial behavior. These make complete sense, even if the universe is deterministic. I discuss these in Chapter 10.

Other Benefits of the Deterministic Worldview May Outweigh Any Erosion of Social Control

Finally, as we will see below, even if afreeism removes some components of social control, it promotes many other prosocial behaviors that may outweigh this loss. An afreeist should be more tolerant and accepting of other people. Social policy based on afreeism will be more humane and effective and thus should promote prosocial outcomes. On a more personal level, by removing some negative emotions, afreeism has the potential to help people to live more joyful productive lives.

The Bottom Line: We Will Be Just Fine

Without feelings of guilt, remorse, or regret, there is some concern that internal social controls may be eroded, which is what I have called the *sinvergüenza problem*. However, we should not be overly concerned. Other potent measures of control—both internal and external continue to exert significant influence. Furthermore, abandoning the idea of desert can lead to profound positive shifts in social policy, in interpersonal relationships, and in self-realization. We will discuss all of these in the following chapters.

Chapter 10

No-fault Crime and Punishment

"Tout comprendre, c'est tout pardonner."
–Leo Tolstoy, War and Peace[74]

FREE WILL HAS LONG BEEN CONSIDERED the very basis of the criminal system. Consider this quote from the 1978 case United States v. Grayson which in turn approvingly cites the 1952 case of Morissette v. United States. The court stated:

> The Scott rationale rests not only on the realism of the psychological pressures on a defendant in the dock— which we can grant—but also on a deterministic view of human conduct that is inconsistent with the underlying precepts of our criminal justice system. A "universal and persistent" foundation stone in our system of law, and particularly in our approach to punishment, sentencing, and incarceration, is the "belief in freedom of the human will and a consequent ability and duty of the normal individual to choose between good and evil." Morissette v. United States, 342 U.S. 246, 250, 72 S.Ct. 240, 243, 96 L.Ed. 288 (1952).[75]

What happens when we realize that free will and moral responsibility are just myths? Dostoevsky in the Grand Inquisitor passage of Brothers Karamozov is eerily prescient:

> Knowest Thou not that, but a few centuries hence, and the whole of mankind will have proclaimed in its wisdom and through its mouthpiece, Science, that there is no more crime, hence no more sin on earth, but only hungry people?[76]

What happens when this "foundation stone" of our system of law disappears? I should say initially that if the entire system of criminal law tumbles into the sea, so be it. Free will is a myth and we need to accept the consequences of knowing that. However, I do not believe that the legal structure is so precarious. It will survive. It will even be better, more efficient, and more humane.

The Afreeist Conundrum

In designing a just and moral society, we are faced with many challenges. Two primary ones are:

1. What should the rules for behavior be?

2. What should be the rewards and punishments for following or deviating from such rules?

In this chapter, I focus on the second question with a particular emphasis on punishment. Punishment presents a difficult problem for the afreeist. Traditionally, we convict someone of a crime only if that person commits the crime of her own free will. Using an example from a previous chapter, we have no problem punishing someone for speeding down the highway. Perhaps the driver wanted to get to an appointment or perhaps just enjoyed the feeling of speed. Such drivers are subject to being pulled over and issued a fine. However, if the driver is driving fast because there is a carjacker holding a gun to her head, then we do not punish. Likewise, if it turns out that the driver had some sort of medical condition unknown to her (for example, a brain tumor) that caused the behavior, we are likely to excuse the illegal action. In these cases, the driver was not speeding of her own free will.

In the deterministic world that we live in, there is no free will. In all three cases above (the speeding driver, the speeding driver with a carjacker, and the speeding driver with a tumor), the fact that the driver is speeding at that very moment is determined by a causal chain that began long ago. How can we punish someone for events that were determined to happen?

And if we cannot punish, what is to become of society? How do we peaceful law-abiding citizens protect ourselves? Of course, punishment is not the only solution to crime. Crime clearly could be significantly reduced, for example, by reducing poverty and inequality and by improving education and healthcare. I will discuss these ideas in the next chapter. In this chapter, I focus on the role of punishment.

Guilt, Revenge, Retribution

In general, rationales for punishment include these:

1. Teaching people moral and legal standards.

2. Exacting retribution from (assigning blame to) those who violate those standards.

3. Deterring people from violating those standards.

4. Incapacitating (removing from general society) people who would likely violate those standards again in the future.

Of the above, the rationale that is most deeply in-grained in us—the one with the deepest evolutionary roots—is retribution.

Retribution

The retributive goal of punishment is, in short, payback. It is the righting of the moral scales whose imbalance was caused by the immoral and illegal actions of the criminal. We evolved to punish those who violate moral and social norms. As Judge Morris Hoffman has observed:

> Evolution built us to punish cheaters. Without that punishment instinct, we would never have been able to live in small groups, and would never have realized all the significant benefits that small-group living conferred, including mutual defense, cooperative hunting, property, divisions of labor, and economies of scale. In fact, to a large extent our notions of right and wrong, of empathy and compassion, of fairness and justice, all come from the tensions of group living, and thus indirectly owe their very existence to punishment.[77]

In a footnote to this paragraph, Hoffman goes on to say:

> Exactly how punishment might have evolved to enable our social living remains a hot topic among evolutionary theorists. Scholars across many disciplines, from evolu-tionary biology and psychology to economics and even neuroscience, seem to be converging on the idea that we needed punishment to help bind us into our extraordinar-ily intense social groups.[78]

Crime and Punishment

Hoffman then continues by pointing out that our brains are wired to implement punishment in three ways:[79]

1. We feel guilt at our own antisocial behavior. (First-party punishment.)

2. We feel the need to retaliate against and to seek revenge from those who harm us. (Second-party punishment.)

3. We feel the need to exact retribution against those who harm others. (Third-party punishment.)

The exacting of punishment is often described in terms of free will:

> ... the essence of punishment is to restrict a criminal's will by depriving him of the right to be the sole author of his own actions. The goal of punishment, in short, is the undoing of the criminal's bold and unjust assertion of his own will.[80]

This type of punishment has deep cerebral roots. As Robert Sapolsky notes, punishing someone for violating moral norms . . .

> ... is a deep, atavistic pleasure Put people in brain scanners, give them scenarios of norm violations. Decision making about culpability for the violation correlates with activity in the cognitive dlPFC. But decision making about appropriate punishment activates the emotional vmPFC, along with the amygdala and insula; the more activation, the more punishment. The decision to punish, the passionate motivation to do so, is a frothy limbic state. . . . Punishment just feels that good.[81]

However, as I noted before, punishment feels good only if we believe that the person who receives the punishment deserves it. Punishing the wrong person, or punishing someone who could not do otherwise, brings no satisfaction.

147

We do not get pleasure from seeing someone punished who acted because of an epileptic seizure, a gun held to her head, or in self-defense.

Of course, because the world is deterministic, *every* act is of this sort. That is, every act is the result of a chain of causation. Retribution is never justified because we could never have done otherwise. Acknowledging that the universe is deterministic should diminish any retributive pleasure from punishment, and it should further remove any consideration of retribution as a justification for punishment.

Other Approaches

Retribution is not the only basis for punishment. Other rationales include education, deterrence, and incapacitation. Nevertheless, because the world is deterministic, all punishments involve the punishment of innocents. So if we are to punish, we must be able to justify the punishment of innocents. Otherwise, we must abandon punishment altogether.

The Public Health Perspective

If we abandon moral responsibility (as we must), we can no longer use this as a basis for punishment. What then? What do we replace it with? Derk Pereboom suggests that, instead of basing the criminal law on moral responsibility, we should base the criminal law on a public health model. Those who commit crimes are not bad people who deserve to be punished. Rather, they are morally sick. Because they are sick, we should try to cure them by providing treatment that will change their moral values. If we fail to cure them, we should quarantine them so that they do no additional harm to society. Using this reasoning, Pereboom suggests that we can justify punishment for education and, in some cases, we can justify removing a person from society.

From this perspective, crime is treated as a serious communicable disease. The criminal and the infected patient both harm those around them. In both cases, this can be remedied through treatment (curing the patient or reforming the criminal) or by removal (quarantining the patient or jailing the criminal). The public health model suggests that we attempt to reform the criminal. Failing that, we are justified in separating the criminal from general society.

The public health model has much to commend it. Basing punishment on a public health model will likely result in more humane treatment of criminals and could be quite effective at reducing antisocial behavior. Under this model, those violating the law should be treated as humanely as possible, consistent with reforming the violator's moral attitudes. Indeed, some programs take this approach and they have been quite effective in reducing recidivism.[82] This approach also implies that, in cases where the individual must be removed from society, we do it humanely. That is, we do our best to give the criminally dangerous person a decent and dignified life. The public health approach permits the punishment and confinement of innocents as long as punishment and confinement are humane.

Nevertheless, there are some differences between contagious illnesses and criminal behavior. In the case of a contagious illness, the sick person typically wants to be cured. The disease has a great impact on the person's well-being and this leads to a desire to accept treatment. Therefore, a sick person usually consents to her treatment. If she does not want to be treated, we do not treat her. In the case of a criminal, the criminal may have no desire to be cured and may not consent to the treatment. (That is, the criminal may not consent to being confined, to paying a fine, or to participating in programs.)

In the case of a serious communicable disease, we may feel justified in giving the sick person a choice: either accept treatment or be quarantined. We may even say that the sick person must be quarantined until she is cured, or at least until she ceases to be contagious. One problem for criminal law is that we do not have good markers as to whether someone is no longer a threat to society. Even the best programs for rehabilitation have significant recidivism rates.

Also, under the public health model, there are only two reasons to lock someone up: re-education or incapacitation. But suppose that re-education is not possible. Imagine someone who, despite attempts at re-education, will drive 20 miles an hour over the speed limit. No matter how much education we subject this person to, she will speed. Because she cannot be re-educated, under the public health model our only option is to incapacitate her, that is, to quarantine her. In other words, we would have either to incarcerate such people or give up on having effective speed limits.

Deterrence

Of course, there is another solution. If we tell the driver that every time she drives over the speed limit there is a 10% chance of a $1000 fine, it may turn out that she stops driving over the speed limit.

Deterrence is not retributive. It seeks simply to change behavior through the application of punishment. However, it comes up against our original problem: the punishment of innocents.

Some who object to deterrence as a basis for punishment ask the following question: would it be acceptable to punish an innocent party if that would deter others from committing a crime? For example, one can imagine a scenario in which a government announces that it has found the perpetrators of a crime, even though it has only arrested innocents, in order to convince the population that if a crime is committed the guilty party will be found and punished. Punishing innocents in this case may reduce crime and make everyone on average better off. That is, the unhappiness of the innocent scapegoats may be offset by the increased happiness of everyone else.

Most people (myself included) would find the above scenario objectionable, even immoral. One might say that to punish the innocent to protect the larger population is wrong. However, since the world is deterministic, if we adopt such a blanket statement, we will have to abandon punishment altogether, because everyone is always innocent. There must be an alternative to this approach. And there is.

First, note that even those who believe in free will accept that the criminal system, if it is to have punishment at all, will inevitably punish innocents. That is, they recognize that sometimes the system will err. Therefore, anyone who argues for punishment of any sort consents to the punishment of some unknown quantity of innocents. The issue is not really whether we should accept the punishment of innocents, but rather under what circumstances. For example, it may be morally justified to punish innocents in error but not intentionally.

But even this formulation leaves us with a conundrum. Because the universe is deterministic, all punishment involves the *intentional* punishment of innocents. Justice Oliver Wendell Holmes, Jr. recognized that punishment meant punishing those we know are innocent to deter others:

> If I were having a philosophical talk with a man I was going to have hanged (or electrocuted) I should say, "I don't doubt that your act was inevitable for you, but to make it more avoidable by others we propose to sacrifice you to the common good. You may regard yourself as a soldier dying for your country if you like."[83]

Given this, the question becomes, are we justified in punishing someone we know to be innocent to deter others? If so, under what circumstances can we do so?

Justifying Punishment

Here again, the public health model might be instructive. Most of us agree that we have the right to quarantine someone to protect the public good. When we quarantine someone, we may be confining them against their will to protect the public, even though we know that such a person is innocent of any wrongdoing. In other words, we are imposing adverse consequences (confinement) on an innocent person for the benefit of society. This, it seems, is morally acceptable. Indeed, it might be immoral to do otherwise.

It is worth pausing for a moment to ask why we feel it is morally justifiable to quarantine an individual against her desires. The answer to this question involves understanding why we ever feel justified in bringing the power of the state to bear on individuals. This has been the subject of much philosophical inquiry. There is no single satisfactory answer to this question, but there are some fruitful lines of inquiry. Before proceeding, however, I want to acknowledge that the following ideas are not without controversy. That said, let us proceed.

Ever since Socrates, philosophers have tried to determine the content of moral and social laws and also have tried to determine when and how the state is justified in enforcing moral and social laws. One mechanism that philosophers often use is social contract theory. This theory dates from the time of Socrates, but it had its first full development by the philosopher Thomas Hobbes (1588-1679). According to social contract theory, we all implicitly enter into a contract with each other and with the sovereign to enact laws that prescribe and proscribe behaviors and specify the consequences if we deviate from those behaviors. Because it is clear that none of us have ever entered into such a contract explicitly (no such form exists with our signatures on it), our agreement is implicit. What does this mean? In a sense, it means that if we were presented with such a contract we would find it in our best interest to sign it. "Our best interest" is broadly defined. We may agree to sign the contract because it benefits us, our families, our friends, or even society at large.

To this theoretical construct, the philosopher John Rawls (1921-2002) added his notion of the "veil of ignorance." This idea suggests that, to evaluate a societal rule involving behavior or consequences, we pretend that we are in the "original position" of not knowing who we will be in society. That is, we are asked to design the rules (write the contract) of society without knowing our gender, sexual orientation or identification, or social class. We do not know our ethnicity, race, or where we will be living. We do not know if we will be tall or short, whether we can walk or are confined to a wheelchair, whether we are sighted or blind. We do not know our intelligence or talents in any particular area. We know nothing of what our personal characteristics or personal history will be. In short, we may be born into this society as anyone. From this original position, behind the veil of ignorance, we must choose our societal rules. Given all this, are there any rules that all of us (or the vast majority of us) would agree on?

Let us apply this idea to the problem at hand. Under such circumstances, would we choose a world in which innocent people with highly contagious and dangerous diseases could be quarantined against their will? Likely, we would, even knowing that we might be that person. However, we would insist on humane conditions for the quarantine.

By the same logic, most of us would likely agree to establish a system of punishment that would operate as a deterrent to the commission of certain harmful acts, even though we acknowledge that we will be intentionally punishing innocent actors in every case, given that, in the deterministic universe, everyone is innocent. We realize in doing so that we may be among those innocent actors who are punished. That is, we justify the imposition of adverse consequences (confinement, fines, etc.) on an innocent person for the benefit of others in society, recognizing that that person could be us. This is just as moral as quarantining an innocent person who has contracted a serious and highly contagious illness.

Limitations on Deterrence

We do, however, want to be careful. For example, it seems

clear that we would never want to endorse punishing those who did not commit the crime just to deter others. There are several reasons for this. First, if we permitted this practice, the deterrent value of punishment would go down because we would never know whether people are being punished arbitrarily or because they committed the act. Second, and perhaps more importantly, we simply should not trust any government with this kind of power for fear that this power would be used for all sorts of nefarious purposes. By prohibiting the deliberate punishment of innocents, we put a check on government power.

Additionally, punishment cannot deter some behaviors. Punishing a speeding driver with a gun to her head will not deter her or others in a similar position. Nor would punishing an action that was caused by a brain tumor. Nor will punishment deter if the action is in response to a higher need, such as self-defense or to protect something of higher personal value. In these cases, deterrence cannot be a justification for punishment. Furthermore, if the person is a compulsive criminal or a sociopath or is otherwise psychologically undeterrable, then deterrence cannot be a justification for punishment. We may, however, be justified in quarantining that person. If we do so, however, it should be done humanely.[84]

Can Free Will and Moral Responsibility Be Justified by Deterrence?

If you accept all of the above, then you might argue that a belief in free will and moral responsibility can reenter the scene through the backdoor of deterrence. That is, even if free will does not exist, could it be that a *belief* in free will (and thus in moral responsibility) will deter people from violating social norms? In other words, blinkered by the veil of ignorance, might we all agree to ignore the evidence against free will and moral responsibility and convince ourselves to believe it? This will serve to deter us. This idea is similar to one argument for the belief in a god. If we could all agree to believe in a god, the belief in that god (whether it corresponds to reality or not) will foster conformance to the moral norms.[85]

Of course, just stating the above proposition reveals its weaknesses. First, it is doubtful that one can simply choose to believe something one knows to be false. Free will and moral responsibility are part of a mythology. This mythology has been under attack for thousands of years, but the last few decades of progress in artificial intelligence and neuroscience have brought new ammunition to bear. The mythology only works if there are believers. As more people accept the deterministic nature of the universe and the nonexistence of free will, the less effective this approach will become.

Second, this mythology is a blunt tool. Although it may deter some bad behavior it can also be the cause of bad behavior. I saw an example of this fairly recently. My wife was on a jury that had to determine whether a convicted sexual predator, call him John, should be released. Years ago John had coerced underage girls into having sex with him. He had been convicted and had served his time—over 30 years. However, under state law, the state could hold John indefinitely if he were found to be a threat to society. John suffered from cerebral palsy which had progressed during the span of his imprisonment. He was confined to a wheelchair, not able to stand up. His limbs shook and he had to be fed. The jury found 11-1 that John should continue to be held and his release was denied. (As this was not a criminal proceeding at this point, John needed a majority decision in his favor to be released.) The attitude of the majority of the jury was expressed by the foreman who said, "If he did that to my daughter, I would lock him up and throw away the key," which is effectively what this jury did.

In the above case, the jury's decision was based on retribution and ignored the law, since John had served his time and posed no threat to society. It is hard to understand how such an outcome benefits society. If the jury had truly understood the deterministic nature of John's actions, they would see that he too is a victim. This is not to say that John should not have been punished. Punishment serves a teaching and a deterrent function. However, keeping John locked up at this point is plainly wrong when retribution is removed from the equation.

Creating mythologies can serve useful purposes, but they can also run amok. Speaking of the mythology of religion, physics Nobel laureate Steven Weinberg wrote:

> Frederick Douglass told in his Narrative how his condition as a slave became worse when his master underwent a religious conversion that allowed him to justify slavery as the punishment of the children of Ham. Mark Twain described his mother as a genuinely good person, whose soft heart pitied even Satan, but who had no doubt about the legitimacy of slavery, because in years of living in antebellum Missouri she had never heard any sermon opposing slavery, but only countless sermons preaching that slavery was God's will. With or without religion, good people can behave well and bad people can do evil; but for good people to do evil—that takes religion.[86]

We see this every day when people who believe they are doing good end up doing harm. Examples of this include young women and men willing to blow themselves and others up, violent attacks on gay and transgender people, and deadly bombings of Planned Parenthood clinics. The religion of free will and moral responsibility can create equally bad outcomes because it is used to justify inhumane retributive policies.

Crime and Punishment Without Free Will

Let us summarize:

1. Because the world is deterministic, there is no free will and no moral responsibility for past actions.

2. Maintaining the myth of free will and moral responsibility is probably not possible in the long-run. There is too much scientific evidence against it. Furthermore, maintaining this myth results in outcomes that often do not serve the social good.

3. Even without the belief in free will and moral responsibility we can create moral rules and justify punishments for violating those rules. The punishments serve to educate and deter. In some cases, confinement can be justified where necessary to protect the public.

Deterrence works because the healthy brain is capable of weighing costs and benefits to various proposed courses of action. Both freeists and afreeists assume this. How do we apply deterrence? Let us look again at the freeist position since that seems to underlie our current conceptions of the criminal law. The freeist position is that if someone commits a crime (robs a bank, say) of her own free will, then she is morally responsible for her actions. That is, she is blameworthy. Because she is blameworthy, we feel justified in punishing her.

Crime and Punishment

The criminal law operationalizes this idea of free will and moral responsibility through a number of doctrines. Two of these are the doctrine of *mens rea* and the defense of compulsion. *Mens rea* is a Latin term meaning "guilty mind," but perhaps is better described as "criminal intent." To win a criminal case, the prosecutor must prove (among other things) *mens rea* beyond a reasonable doubt. It makes a difference to the criminal law whether one acts purposefully, knowingly, recklessly, or negligently. For most criminal offenses, if someone commits a prohibited act intending the results of that act, then one has committed the act purposefully and (if the other elements of the crime are proven) is guilty of a criminal offense. If someone shoots and kills someone with the intent to kill her, then the shooter is guilty of a criminal offense. Likewise, if a bank robber detonates a safe, not for the purpose of killing someone (since the bank robber is only interested in the money), but knowing that the bank employee sitting near the safe will be killed, then the bank robber is guilty of murder. Taking an action that will purposefully or knowingly kill someone is defined as murder.

Mental state makes a big difference in the criminal law. Consider the following variations of someone (a driver) who kills someone else (a victim) by running her over in a car:

1. The driver intends to kill the victim.

2. The driver is drunk and impaired. The driver does not intend to kill anyone.

3. The driver is not drunk or impaired but is operating the vehicle negligently, perhaps driving 50 mph in a 25-mph school zone. The driver does not intend to kill anyone.

4. The driver is old and infirm with poor eyesight and slow reaction time. The driver does not see the victim in time and unintentionally kills her.

159

5. The driver is driving fast at the point of a gun. The driver loses control, running over and killing the victim.

6. The driver is driving reasonably for the conditions and obeying all laws. Nevertheless, the driver suffers a stroke in the car, loses control, and kills the victim.

7. The driver is driving reasonably for the conditions and obeying all laws. Nevertheless, the victim runs out in front of the car, is struck, and dies.

The law treats each of these situations differently. The traditional freeist rationale is that the examples represent different levels of moral culpability.

The afreeist, however, recognizes that all of these cases were the result of deterministic causal chains in which no free will was operating. For this reason, none of the actors have any degree of moral responsibility. Nevertheless, we can analyze these cases on the basis of deterrence and incapacitation. In the first case, where the driver intends to kill the victim, deterrence plays a big role. In a world in which there are consequences for committing murder, we would expect fewer murders. We could all agree that, in this example, the driver should face serious consequences.

In the drunk driving case we would like to provide incentives 1) not to get so drunk and 2) once drunk, not to get behind the wheel of a car and 3) once drunk and behind the wheel of a car, to drive very carefully. By punishing drunk driving we probably influence all three behaviors. Likewise, negligent driving (Case 3) can be deterred through fines, imprisonment, and compensation to the victims.

As for someone who is old and infirm, incapacitation might be the most rational response to the above event. We suspend the driver's license. We also might require more frequent tests for licensing. Those with abnormally slow reactions, poor eyesight, etc., would not be able to get their licenses renewed.

In cases 5 through 7, there is no need for deterrence and therefore no need to punish.

The bottom line is that many aspects of the criminal justice system will not change. But our thinking about criminal law should change in some important ways. I discuss these in the next section.

Criminal Justice Reform

The main benefit in recognizing the deterministic nature of the universe is that, by abandoning the notions of free will, moral responsibility, and retribution, we can get on with reforming the criminal justice system.

The criminal justice system in the United States needs reform. We imprison people far too often and for far too long. The International Centre for Prison Studies reports that 714 persons per 100,000 population are currently imprisoned in the United States.[87] U.S. prisons are barbaric, violent, dehumanizing institutions. Inmates are regularly humiliated and brutalized. The Equal Justice Initiative, a non-profit that works for prison reform in Alabama reports that,

> The warehousing of one in 100 Americans has all but eradicated rehabilitative programs, and the conditions of confinement in jails, prisons, and detention facilities have dramatically worsened. In 2011, conditions became so "horrendous" in California—home to some of the country's harshest "Three Strikes, You're Out" enhanced sentencing laws—that the United States Supreme Court in Brown v. Plata required the state to release up to 46,000 prisoners after finding that its severely overcrowded

prisons and grossly inadequate medical and mental health care is "incompatible with the concept of human dignity and has no place in civilized society."

About 75,000 people in the United States are held in solitary confinement, spending 23 or more hours a day in small cells, allowed out only for showers, brief exercise, or medical visits, without telephone calls or visits from family members. The use of long-term isolation escalated after "tough on crime" policies led states to build super-maximum-security prisons in the 1980s and 1990s. Studies show that people held in long-term solitary confinement suffer from anxiety, paranoia, perceptual disturbances, and deep depression. Nationwide, suicides among people held in isolation, who make up 3 to 8 percent of the nation's prison population, account for about 50 percent of prison suicides.[88]

This barbarism has many sources, but retribution is likely primary among them. Once a person is found guilty, particularly of violent crimes, that person is deprived of her humanity. The convict gets what she "deserves," no matter how dehumanizing and brutal the treatment.

If we understand the causal determinism of the universe, we also understand that we cannot justify this treatment. The commission of the crime was determined by factors that were in place long before the criminal was born. How can such a person be responsible for her actions?

Realizing that the universe is deterministic should help us empathize both with the offender and with those harmed by the offender. It should release us from that "frothy limbic state"[89] referred to earlier in this chapter, the agitated emotional state our brains are in when we administer punishment to those who we believe deserve it. Instead, we would apply punishment reluctantly, grudgingly, and even sparingly. Above all, we try to do it rationally, all the time realizing that there, but for the grace of the universe, go I. We should be asking what is the least amount of punishment that will produce an acceptable amount of deterrence? Can we use this opportunity to teach the offender (and others in society) moral, social, or civic values? As a last resort, perhaps the offender is dangerous and cannot be reformed. In that case, we may have to separate the offender from the rest of society. But if we do, we must do so humanely.

This is not a book on the particulars of criminal justice system reform. The takeaway points of this chapter are these:

1. The criminal system will not collapse once one realizes that (a) the universe unfolds deterministically and (b) because of this, people are not morally responsible for what they do. Deterrence, rehabilitation, and incapacitation continue to make sense as morally justifiable bases for punishment.

2. The mistaken notions of free will and moral responsibility have led to the acceptance of retribution as a rationale for punishment. This has contributed to the brutality and inhumanity of our current criminal justice system. (This criticism applies to compatibilist defenses of free will and moral responsibility as much as to the libertarian defenses.)

3. By jettisoning the concepts of free will and moral responsibility, we can create a criminal justice system that makes sense. Punishments will be fewer and less severe than under the current system, prisons will become humane institutions, and we will put increasing resources into rehabilitation.

Conclusion

As this book is going to press, the case of R. Kelly is in the news. R. Kelly (a tremendously gifted and successful musician) was the subject of the Lifetime television series, Surviving R. Kelly. The series chronicled a series of abusive relationships that R. Kelly had with underage girls. How should we look at this? In a deterministic world, what happened had to happen. There is no blame, just victims. It is perhaps noteworthy that R. Kelly himself was the victim of abuse as a child. But this is irrelevant to the issue of whether R. Kelly deserves blame. Whether or not R. Kelly was abused, his actions were the result of a causal chain.

If R. Kelly is found to have sexually abused underage girls, then he should be punished. That punishment will deter others from engaging in similar activities in the future. The sentence that R. Kelly receives should also include measures to improve his behavior once he is out of confinement. That is, we should attempt to rehabilitate R. Kelly by teaching him to follow moral and social norms. In designing the punishment, we should make it as humane and rehabilitative as possible, consistent with our desire to deter. Retribution—locking him up in a brutal and inhumane prison for years because that is what he "deserves" —should not be part of the equation.

Chapter 11

Wealth and Poverty

IN A MODERN ECONOMY, people work, almost always collectively, to produce goods and services. The process creates income and wealth. The economic system affects what goods and services are produced, how they are produced and by whom, and how they are distributed to members of society. Economic policy is therefore key to the achievement of a good society, a society that we would like to live in.

We must make choices about how our economy is organized. Some of us do so directly. That is, we may work for the government and be involved in policy decisions. At a minimum, most of us can vote.

There is no such thing as a completely laissez-faire position when it comes to economic policy. If one believes in markets, for example, then we must put into place the institutional underpinnings of a market economy. Such an economy needs the concept of private property and the means to protect property rights. This means it needs property rules, the courts, and the police. And even the most ardent marketeers concede that there are some products and services, such as national defense, that the government should provide. Others believe that the government should have a role in infrastructure creation and maintenance, such as in the area of transportation (roads and bridges), the power grid, and the internet.

Many members of society would encourage additional governmental intervention. They support regulation, such as the highly successful Clean Air Act, the provision of medical insurance under Medicaid and Medicare, and retirement funding under Social Security. People differ in their viewpoints regarding the level of funding and the breadth of government involvement, but a considerable number of people support minimum wage laws, the regulation of medicines, and food labeling.

In other words, we as a society have decisions to make. One thing we need to decide is how we distribute the benefits of the economic system. Although afreeism has little to say about specific policies, it does provide a valuable principle as a starting point. This principle, which I discussed in Chapter 8, is the Equality Principle. Here it is again:

1. Unless there are reasons for doing otherwise, the costs and benefits of society should be distributed equally.

2. Deservedness cannot be a reason for distributing the costs and benefits of society unequally.

The equality principle comes from the afreeist conclusion that there is no such thing as deservedness. Because the world is deterministic, successes and failures are just the product of a causal web. Outcomes could not have been otherwise so no one deserves anything.

Deservedness cannot be a reason to deviate from equality. However, there may be reasons other than deservedness not to distribute wealth and income equally. We should scrutinize and analyze these reasons carefully. I will argue that deviations from equality should be modest. Unfortunately, they are not.

Measuring Societal Benefits Correctly

Having equality of benefits does not mean everyone will end up with identical baskets of goods and services. People have different values and will choose (deterministically) the desired contents of their basket among those items available. For example, some people value leisure more than others, or value leisure more during some times in their lives than in other times. If we look only at goods and services, we might observe inequality, but if we factor in that some people are working harder than others then we might see less inequality.

In other words, leisure has value and some people may choose more leisure over more income. The value of leisure that they are getting compensates for the lower income. Suppose, for example, that we can put a dollar value on leisure. Now consider the following hypothetical distribution:

	Value of Goods and Services Consumed	Value of Leisure Consumed	Total Value
Abby	200	800	1000
Bob	900	100	1000

Abby is retired and gets a tremendous benefit from not having to get up and go to work every day. Leisure is worth a lot to her and she consumes a lot of it. Bob, on the other hand, is working two jobs and gets very little time for leisure. Perhaps he is early in his career and wishes to get ahead quickly. If we look at just the value of goods and services, we would conclude that benefits are distributed unequally. However, looking at total value, including leisure, we see that benefits are equally distributed.

In addition, people have different ways of distributing the consumption of goods, services, and leisure over their lifetimes. Some may prefer more consumption now and less later; others may have the opposite preference.

The difficulty of assigning value complicates matters. Some goods are priced by the market, so at least at the margins, we have an estimate of value. Other goods, such as clean air or a crime-free neighborhood, are more difficult to price. Even with market goods, extreme maldistribution of buying power means that the market prices of many goods do not represent their value, especially to those who cannot afford them.

All of this is to say that the measurement of societal benefits is not easy. Nevertheless, we may be able to draw some rough conclusions.

Inequality in the United States

Despite the difficulty in measuring societal benefits, it is not hard to conclude that the distribution of benefits in the United States and the world is grossly unequal. Many live in poverty while others live in opulence. So much income and wealth are concentrated in the top one percent (and one-tenth of one percent) of the population that, if we distributed income and wealth better, we could eliminate world poverty. In this country (and many more) the tax system exacerbates poverty. (As Warren Buffet has famously said, his secretary pays a greater percentage of her income in taxes than he does.[90]) Wealth and income also have a racial dimension. African-Americans and Latinos have far lower income and wealth than whites. Here are some facts for the United States:

- As of 2019, over 35 million people live in food-insecure households, including over 5 million children.[91]

- As of 2019, the three wealthiest individuals in this country (Bezos, Gates, and Buffet) have more wealth than the bottom 50% of the population (over 160 million people).[92]

- Currently, the top 400 richest people in this country (.00025 percent of the population) now have more wealth than the bottom 63% of the population (over 200 million people).[93]

- Among families in the United States, the top 1% have almost twice as much wealth as the bottom 90% of families. This is concentrated in the top 0.1% of families who have approximately the same amount of wealth as the bottom 90% of all families.[94]

- Median family wealth, when measured by race, is very unequal: White—$171,000; Black—$17,150; Latinx—$20,720.[95] (These are conservative estimates. Other estimates show even greater disparities.[96])

Afreeism says that we cannot justify these disparities by deservedness. So, the question is whether any other justification exists for such disparities.

Equality and Efficiency

One justification for inequality is that a certain amount of inequality increases the size of the pie. It does so by creating incentives. This could be beneficial for everyone. To see this, consider the following two distributions:

	Distribution A	Distribution B
Abby	100	2000
Bob	100	1500
Chris	100	1700
Danielle	100	1300
Evert	100	1900

Note that I am assuming that we are measuring benefit using the same units in the two distributions, something akin to buying power.

In Distribution A, the benefits of society are distributed equally. I would guess that the members of this society would prefer Distribution B, in which all are better off, despite the distribution not being equal. In other words, societal welfare is a function of both the size of the pie and how the pie is divvied up. Perhaps the reason why Distribution B results in such a larger pie, is that the system that underlies it provides incentives for productive work. If so, then this has to be taken into account.

On the other hand, efficiency is not the sole criterion. In some cases, we would be willing to accept a little smaller pie in exchange for it being divided more equally. For example, consider these distributions:

	Distribution A	Distribution B
Abby	2000	100
Bob	2100	100
Chris	2000	100
Danielle	1900	100
Evert	2000	10,000
Sum of Benefits	**10,000**	**10,400**

Most people would prefer Distribution A to Distribution B, especially if they chose from behind the "veil of ignorance," that is, without knowing who they would be in this distribution.

This indicates that the size of the pie may be important, but it is not everything. There is a trade-off between equality and efficiency. We are willing to give up some equality for greater efficiency and some efficiency for greater equality.

Incentives

We have already determined that the distribution of resources should not be based on who deserves it. In the deterministic universe, no one deserves anything. However, we also concluded that we are willing to sacrifice some equality for measures that increase the size of the pie significantly. Incentives are one way to increase the size of the pie. That is, we give rewards to those who are willing to educate themselves, work, and take reasonable risks.

So, the question becomes, how unequal must the distribution of societal benefits be to provide reasonable incentives for efficiency? This is not easy to quantify precisely. It depends on knowing how much additional output greater incentives will produce, how much societal value this additional output will provide, how much equality will be sacrificed, and how much we value that loss of equality. The question is difficult, but let's take a stab at answering it.

First, note that the current level of inequality in the United States is staggering. Again, the top 1% of families have more wealth than the entire bottom 90%. The 400 richest people in the U.S. have more wealth than the bottom 63%. The top three wealthiest people have more wealth than the entire bottom 50% of the population. Here are the top five wealthiest people in the United States as of February 2021:[97]

	Wealth	**Primary Source**
Elon Musk	$203 billion	Tesla
Jeff Bezos	$195 billion	Amazon
Bill Gates	$135 billion	Microsoft
Benard Arnault	$113 billion	Dior
Mark Zuckerberg	$102 billion	Facebook

Income is also highly unequal. For example, here are the incomes for 2019 for the top-earning hedge-fund managers in the United States: [98]

	Firm	Income	Net Worth
Christopher Hohn	TCI Fund Mgt	$1.8 Billion	$5 Billion
James Simons	Renaissance Tech	$1.8 Billion	$23.5 Billion
Ken Griffen	Citadel	$1.5 Billion	$15 Billion
Israel Englander	Millennium Mgt	$1.5 Billion	$7.2 Billion
Chase Coleman	Tiger Global Mgt	$1.4 Billion	$6.9 Billion

In the meantime, almost 35 million people in the United States live in food-insecure households. Almost 14% of households with children are food insecure.[99] One child in thirty will experience homelessness at some time during a given calendar year.[100]

The question is, can such inequality of income and wealth be justified by incentives? A couple of thought experiments should make the answer to this question fairly obvious.

1. Suppose that you had told the young Jeff Bezos, before he ever started working on what would become Amazon, that he stood to gain, say, $10 billion in personal wealth if Amazon were successful instead of the nearly $200 billion that he is currently worth. Would he have made the same efforts? (Clearly, the answer is yes.)

2. Suppose you had told hedge fund manager James Simons in 2018 that his income would be 90% lower, a mere $160 million for the year. Would he have refused to go to work? (No.) If you had told him before he ever became a hedge fund manager, that his top salary would be $160 million a year or lower, would that have deterred him? (No.)

Of course, you do not have to be an afreeist to be troubled by the extremes of wealth and poverty. Nor do you have to be an afreeist to conclude that these extremes cannot be justified by incentives. What afreeism brings to the table is that these extremes cannot be justified by deservedness either. None of these very wealthy people deserve what they got. Nor do people deserve to live in poverty.

In a way, this is another facet of what we discussed in Chapter 8 on criminal law. We should not inflict retribution on people because, given that the universe is deterministic, people do not *deserve* punishment. Likewise, people do not deserve abject poverty or unspeakable wealth. However, just as in the criminal law we tolerate some punishment for the sake of deterring bad behavior and protecting society, we may want to tolerate some inequality for the sake of creating incentives. In the case of criminal law, we should seek to minimize punishment to a level that still provides adequate safety for the population. Likewise, with broader social policy we should seek to minimize inequality to a level that provides adequate incentives.

Fixing Inequality

Detailed policy recommendations on how to fix the massive inequality in the United States and the world are beyond the scope of this book. But we can sketch out some ideas.

For a start, we could tax the incomes of Jeff Bezos and hedge fund manager James Simon at significantly higher rates. The current system in the United States is perverse in this regard. Someone who makes $60,000 a year pays a greater share of her income in taxes than someone who makes more than $1 million when all taxes (income, payroll, sales, etc.) are taken into account. Wealth taxes should also be on the table, as should laws increasing the minimum wage. Universal health care (depending on how it is paid for) could also mitigate wealth disparities, as would a more robust social security system.

Money raised using progressive income taxes or wealth taxes could be used to reduce poverty through subsidies such as the Earned Income Tax Credit or through the provision of services, such as health services and investments in public education.

These are just some ideas. Afreeism does not directly favor one policy over another. Rather, the afreeist perspective provides us with concrete goals that should guide our societal choices. There is much hard work to be done to figure which policies will help transform the economy to one that more fairly distributes costs and benefits.

The Bottom Line

As we look forward to the future through the lens of causation we can see that what we do makes a difference. Although afreeism is not a political philosophy, it does teach us to look at the world differently. Once we discard the blinders of deservedness, we see with clarity how unjustified it is for some to have so much wealth while others live in such poverty. No one deserves these consequences at either end of the spectrum.

Chapter 12

Afreeist Freedom

WARS HAVE BEEN FOUGHT in the name of freedom. Songs have been written proclaiming it. "My country 'tis of thee, sweet land of liberty . . . let freedom ring." The United States national anthem affirms that America is "the land of the free." New Hampshire license plates scream, "Live free or die!" Dylan asked, "Yes, 'n' how many years can some people exist before they're allowed to be free?"

The market economy rests on the so-called freedom of exchange. As the theory goes, individuals know better than anyone else what they value. If I value apples more than oranges and you value oranges more than apples, and if we can freely trade, then I can trade one of my oranges for one of your apples. Having the freedom to make that trade makes us both better off.

Freedom also makes government and other institutions function better. Freedom of speech, freedom of the press, and the freedom to assemble allows us to communicate with our government and with other institutions, to express dissatisfaction with their policies. Freedom of religion and freedom from religion allow us the satisfaction of following our beliefs.

There is an ongoing philosophical debate on whether freedom is important in itself, and not just because it allows individuals to maximize their personal benefits by choosing among alternatives. In other words, perhaps it just feels good to think yourself free.

But are we truly free at all? Does freedom exist in a deterministic universe?

Types of Freedom

We cannot change the fact that the universe is deterministic. If this implies that we do not have freedom, so be it. However, freedom is relative and what we mean by freedom is relative. Although we are constrained by causal factors, these factors have different characteristics. Much of the discussion around freedom has to do with types of constraints, not on whether people are constrained.

For example, there is a large debate framed around positive freedom and negative freedom. Negative freedom is defined as "freedom from" and positive freedom as "freedom to." In particular, those touting negative freedom see it as freedom from restrictions on action imposed by other human beings, particularly by governments. Any form of restriction imposed on an individual by a government reduces negative freedom. Positive freedom, on the other hand, looks at a wider array of constraints on action. For example, someone who has fewer of society's resources has fewer options as to what and how much to consume. They are less free in the positive sense.

These two freedoms are often in conflict. Consider the following distributions:

	Distribution A	Distribution B
Abby	500	600
Bob	600	700
Chris	500	700
Danielle	700	800
Evert	400	600

Suppose that Distribution A represents a fairly unregulated economy. The economy produces positives (food, shelter, etc.) and negatives (pollution, etc.). Suppose that the government steps in and regulates air quality and provides financial incentives for research and development, such as a patent system that restricts the ability of competitors to use patented technology for many years. As a result, suppose that the economy improves, as represented by Distribution B. Not only do the members of our society get cleaner air, they also get access to a greater number of products. In this case, negative freedom declined, due to increased government restrictions, but positive freedom increased.

Proponents of negative freedom do not recognize positive freedom as freedom. For them, only negative freedom is freedom. Isaiah Berlin states,

> If I say that I am unable to jump more than ten feet in the air, or cannot read because I am blind, or cannot understand the darker pages of Hegel, it would be eccentric to say that I am to that degree enslaved or coerced. Coercion implies the deliberate interference of other human beings within the area in which I could otherwise act.[101]

According to Berlin, merely not having enough resources to buy something is not a lack of liberty. Berlin, and others, did realize that negative liberty is not absolute. Liberty could indeed be traded off against other values, such as a fairer distribution of resources. What he objected to was calling this an increase in freedom, even though many members of the society would have more alternatives available to them.

Of course, others disagree with Berlin. Picture subjects being put in a room with a vendor of goods. Suppose that these goods are priced as follows:

Good A: $10

Good B: $20

Good C: $30

Now consider two subjects. Subject 1 is given $10 and told to buy whatever she wants. Subject 2 is given $30 and told that the government has prohibited the sale of Good B, but other than that she can purchase whatever she wants. Who is most free? One who believes that only negative freedom is freedom would say Subject 1 is freer, because there are no governmental restrictions. Those who argue for freedom as defined by positive freedom would say Subject 2 is most free, because she has access to Goods A and C, whereas Subject 1 has access only to Good A.

Types of Constraints

Now what does determinism have to say about this? First, because all decisions are completely determined, we might conclude that we have no freedom. And, in a sense, we would be right.

However, freedom is more complicated. The above discussion on positive and negative freedom is instructive. When we talk about freedom, we are not talking about absolutes. When someone says that she is free, she is not saying that she is free to flap her arms and fly away. Freedom refers to a lack of particular constraints. For example, when we say that we have political freedom, we are saying that the government is not constraining us unduly. When we say that we have economic freedom, we are saying that a lack of resources is not constraining us. Thus, we may possess political freedom or economic freedom in the deterministic universe.

To see how freedom differs from free will, imagine that we create a robot and give it a certain latitude of movement. We could confine it to a 4-foot by 4-foot room. This would limit its freedom of movement. Or we could limit it to a 12-foot by 12-foot room. Or we could let it go outside. In each case, there is a certain amount of freedom of movement. We could have debates about how much freedom of movement the robot should have.

Notice that we are talking about the freedom of a robot to move about even though we would never say that the robot has free will. The robot's actions are still deterministic. Even if we give it unlimited freedom of movement, it may never go outside the original 4-foot by 4-foot area because other causal factors, including its programming, are constraining it.

Freedom, then, refers to freedom from a particular constraint. Imagine a world in which an action is completely determined by a combination of the following constraints:

Political constraint

Resource constraint

Mobility constraint

Suppose that a person deterministically acts to maximize pleasure subject to these constraints. Some of these constraints may be binding; that is, the person bumps into them. Others may not be binding either because the maximization of pleasure does not lead to the person to bumping into the constraint or other constraints come into play first. We can tell if a constraint is binding by contemplating what would happen if we removed it. If removing it would change the subject's action, then it is binding. Otherwise, it is not.

In our simple world, freedom from government restrictions involves removing or reducing the political constraint. This may or may not affect behavior. Economic freedom would involve removing or reducing the resource constraint. Again, this may or may not affect behavior.

It should be clear that one can put the label of freedom on the removal or reduction of any constraint. For example, giving wheelchairs to people in poor countries who cannot afford them (reducing the mobility constraint), as one NGO does, increases tremendously the freedom of those receiving the wheelchairs.

Afreeist Freedom

If we design a robot and give it a task—for example, to maximize some goal—the amount of freedom of movement we give it may affect the extent to which it accomplishes its goal. Suppose we have a robot that we give the task of collecting used containers for recycling. Let's begin by confining the robot to a one-block area and a twenty-four-hour time limit. If we increase the robot's freedom of movement to, say, ten blocks and its freedom of time to, say, one week, we may get better results. The same principle applies to humans. Furthermore, humans may actually value freedom even if the results in terms of other societal benefits are the same. The fact that we give the robot more freedom of movement, does not mean that the robot's actions are not determined—they are, and so are the human's actions—yet we may be happier and more productive with greater freedom (fewer constraints).

Afreeist freedom involves the removal of constraints on action. When a binding constraint is removed, other constraints usually become binding so the removal of that restraint may or may not make us happier. For example, if I allow my young daughter to purchase concert tickets (removing the parental constraint), she then is faced with a monetary constraint that may limit her ability to buy the tickets or to get good seats. She may actually find this more frustrating than the parental constraint.

Nevertheless, the removal of constraints has the potential to make us happier. For example, removing a constraint on the exchange of goods allows us to trade less valuable goods for more valuable goods. Removing constraints on political speech may result in greater governmental accountability resulting in better government action that benefits more of us. It may also result in the exchange of ideas that further social and scientific progress. Removing constraints on the practice of religion may result in activity that brings us greater satisfaction.

We may decide to trade some freedoms for others, or even trade some freedoms off against other important social goals. The freedom to assault our neighbor may be traded off for the right to be free from assault. The freedom to pollute may be traded off against freedom from pollution. The freedom to monopolize may be traded off against the freedom to compete in an open competitive market.

Afreeism recognizes that these freedoms exist and are important.

We can imagine two different robot societies, one in which the robots are free to speak, exchange goods, and travel about, and another where the robots cannot do these things. Allowing the robots in the first robot world these freedoms may result in a better, more thriving robot society. Yet, both robot worlds are completely deterministic. None of the robots have free will.

In our deterministic world, freedom can exist even though free will does not. Freedom is just the absence of constraints on action. Nothing more... but also nothing less.

Chapter 13

Other Social Policy

IN THE LAST THREE CHAPTERS we looked at criminal law, issues of wealth and poverty, and afreeist conceptions of freedom. Recognizing that the world is deterministic influences our perceptions as to what is good social policy. In this chapter, I look at how the afreeist perspective might influence how we approach a few other issues, including foreign policy, policies on immigration, and policies regulating discrimination.

Foreign Policy

In the area of criminal law, we learned that moral desert is incompatible with determinism. Retribution is always and everywhere unjustified. The same reasoning applies to foreign policy. We know from history that blame and retribution have formed the basis of some of the worst foreign policy decisions and some of the worst atrocities of the twentieth century. For example, the treaty of Versailles, which ended the First World War, placed the blame for the war squarely on Germany. The terms of the treaty exacted retribution in the form of reparations, lost territory, and draconian restrictions on economic activity. This policy was a major contributing factor to the Second World War.

In that war, six million Jews—two-thirds of the Jewish population of Europe—were murdered. Although there were various motivations, at least part of the rationalization was retribution for the alleged role of Jews in the German surrender in the First World War and their alleged role in the subsequent economic depression following the war.

Retribution was also a primary factor in the Rwanda genocide. Local minority Tutsis were blamed both for internal problems and external problems (including a war with external Tutsi rebels). The catalyst for the genocide was the shooting down of the Hutu president's plane. As the BBC reported:

> In Kigali, the presidential guard immediately initiated a campaign of retribution. Leaders of the political opposition were murdered, and almost immediately, the slaughter of Tutsis and moderate Hutus began.[102]

Evidence shows that the genocide had been planned much earlier. The shooting down of the plane provided the retributive trigger. During the Rwanda genocide between 800,000 and 1,000,000 Tutsis were murdered, roughly 70% of the Tutsi population of Rwanda. The slaughter of Tutsis ended when a Tutsi rebel group gained control of the capital. Following this, around 100,000 Hutus were killed in acts of revenge.

Foreign policy is complex. Looking at it from a deterministic vantage point does not reduce this complexity. It does counsel for the following, however:

1. Retribution should not be a factor in foreign policy decision-making. In particular, the use of force should not be based on retribution. As with criminal law, there may be other rationales for the use of force, including deterrence and incapacitation.

2. A causal model of the universe should reinforce our motivation to examine the causes of any potential conflict. All conflicts and potential conflicts have causes.

With this in mind, we can strive for a foreign policy that is more humane and thoughtful.

Development Aid

In Chapter 11 we discussed issues of wealth and poverty in the United States. However, the principles discussed in that chapter apply worldwide. There is absolutely no reason why some people deserve to be rich and others poor.

How can we justify such extremes in wealth and poverty in the world? Frankly, we cannot. The fact that the world is deterministic implies the Equality Principle. Again, the *Equality Principle* is the following moral imperative:

1. Unless there are reasons for doing otherwise, the costs and benefits of society should be distributed equally.

2. Deservedness cannot be a reason for distributing the costs and benefits of society unequally.

Applied worldwide, we should be striving for a distribution of societal (in this case, worldly) benefits that is as equal as possible, consistent with incentives to keep the pie reasonably large. As discussed before, this means that equality is not everything. But neither is efficiency. We should be willing to trade off a little equality for policies that make the pie significantly bigger. Likewise, we should be willing to trade off a little efficiency for policies that make the distribution of income and wealth significantly more equal.

As with the maldistribution of wealth and income in the United States, extreme inequality in wealth and income in the world cannot be justified by incentives. We could significantly reduce the amount of inequality and still provide powerful incentives for work and risk.

What does this mean in terms of policy? First, as a nation, we should be giving much more money away. The foreign aid development budget of the United States, which provides money and resources for economic development in developing countries, is currently less than 0.2% of GDP. As a society, we need to have a serious discussion aimed at determining the proper number, but less than 0.2% is not enough.

Immigration

There is nearly unanimous agreement among policymakers that the immigration system needs major reform. What does afreeism say about immigration? First, as everyone recognizes (not just afreeists), one does not choose where one is born. One does not deserve to be born in a developed country; nor does one deserve to be born in a less developed country.

Yet many people in developed countries believe that it is right to exclude others from the opportunities and benefits that come from being born in a developed country. It is unclear where this feeling of entitlement originates.

Afreeism teaches us that no one deserves anything ever. The resultant Equality Principle counsels us to promote equality unless there is a compelling reason not to do so. Deservedness is not a reason.

One way to promote equality of opportunity and benefits is through a generous immigration policy. This policy would allow as much immigration as possible consistent with maintaining an orderly and productive system. The Equality Principle can be reframed in the immigration context:

1. Unless there are reasons for doing otherwise, people should have the freedom to move wherever they want.

2. Deservedness cannot be a reason for limiting freedom of movement.

Many immigrants are fleeing poverty and crime in the countries where they were born. Many immigrants currently at the southern border of the United States, for example, have had family members murdered by gangs, and have been threatened with being killed themselves. Others are simply seeking economic opportunity in a place where they can raise their families in peace and provide their children with good nutrition, good shelter, and good education.

There is no good reason why we should not open our borders to many more immigrants than we do now, to families who are fleeing oppression, violence, and poverty and who are seeking a better life. Naturally, we should do so in a controlled way, to provide the kind of functioning economy that benefits everyone. We, in the United States and in many other countries of the developed world, have the resources to do so. We should be as generous with those resources as possible. There but for the grace of the universe go we.

Note that the immigration issue is related to two others. First, the issue of immigration is related to the issue of inequality in the United States. Because of the extreme inequality in the United States, there is a significant amount of poverty. Even the middle classes have lifestyles that are significantly worse than they could be if income and wealth were more fairly distributed. Because many people see immigration as further eroding their economic and social positions, they oppose it. In contrast, those who are better off tend to support more generous immigration policies.[103] We can conclude, then, that if we address the extreme inequality in income and wealth in the United States, and thereby raise incomes for the vast majority of residents, there should be greater popular support of a more generous immigration policy.

There is also an important relationship between immigration and development. Most immigrants do not leave their countries of origin—countries where they grew up, where they have family, relatives, and friends, countries where they speak the language and value the culture—without good reason. Most are fleeing poverty and violence. Development aid can improve living conditions, increase economic opportunity, reduce crime, and increase safety in many of these countries. That is, development aid can reduce the demand for immigration. In the run-up to the 2020 United States presidential election, several candidates recognized this interconnection. One even called for a Marshall Plan for Central America.[104]

Anti-Discrimination Policy

That the world is deterministic implies that we should treat people equally unless we have a good reason to do otherwise. This is just an application of the Equality Principle. There are many areas in which even freeists believe that the world operates in accordance with some 'deterministic' factors. Race and ethnicity are clearly determined by physical, biological, and social factors.

There are other areas where the popular view is more varied. For example, science tells us that sexual orientation is biologically determined. Yet some doubt this, preferring to believe that it is a matter of choice.

Afreeism holds that nothing is a matter of free choice. This knowledge that everything is determined can affect how accepting of others we are. For example, a 2010 study showed that people who believed that LGBTQ orientation was biologically determined were more tolerant towards LGBTQ people than those who believed that orientation was a matter of choice.[105] Understanding that the world is deterministic should lead people to be more accepting of others.

Afreeism does not imply that we should never discriminate. Discriminating means treating different people differently. We may be justified on grounds of deterrence, for example, in discriminating between those who have committed a crime and those who have not. However, afreeism and the resultant Equality Principle require that any discrimination be justified. It also limits the types of justifications that can be used. Afreeism specifies that discrimination cannot be based on the idea that a person *deserves* some disparate treatment.

Anti-discrimination laws embody some of these ideals. For the most part, these laws embrace the deterministic nature of race, gender, and sexual orientation. Of course, controversies remain.

Affirmative Action

Affirmative action allows race and gender to be considered in hiring decisions and, in the case of universities, admissions decisions. Proponents of affirmative action justify it in at least two ways. One is that the policy corrects the effects of past discrimination. Suppose our societal goal is one of equal opportunity. This comports with the Equality Principle. Consider a group of people born in 1992. Suppose that we would like people born in 1992 to all have the same opportunity of getting into Harvard eighteen or so years later, irrespective of their gender, race, or sexual orientation. (Note that we are addressing equality of opportunity here; not equality of outcome.) If we subsequently give one group (say, whites) the advantages of good nutrition, good pre-school, and good primary and secondary educations, and give another group (say, African-Americans) poor nutrition, poor pre-school, primary, and secondary educations, then we have violated our principle of equal opportunity by increasing the probabilities of one group attending Harvard and lowering those of the other. Through affirmative action, however, we can readjust the probabilities to give all people born in 1992, the same probability (measured at the time of their birth) to attend Harvard.

The second justification of affirmative action, at least in university admissions, is that it is good for all students to go to school in a diverse environment, where they can rub elbows with others who do not look like them and whose life experiences differ from theirs.

Those who oppose affirmative action often demand that university admissions be solely merit-based. These arguments are often predicated on the notion that students who worked hard and excelled in high school, deserve to have their efforts rewarded.

Of course, to an afreeist, merit is just as determined as race. There is no sense in which anyone deserves to have her efforts rewarded. No one, of any race or ethnic group, deserves to get into Harvard. Any merit-based system has to be justified by other rationales. One rationale may be incentives. However, it is doubtful that affirmative action significantly reduces incentives, so some other justification is required. Since affirmative action increases the equality of opportunity, the burden of proof is on those who oppose affirmative action to justify their position.

Last Words on Afreeist Social Policy

The main principle of this chapter is that, because the universe is deterministic, we are where we are due to causes for which that we cannot take credit. We neither deserve our good fortune nor are to blame for our poor fortune. Where we were born, what we look like, how intelligent or creative we happen to be, what kind of education we got, and even our capacity for hard work, are all determined. Indeed, there is no moral reason why we should be better off or worse off than others. The default arrangement should be equality.

Of course, there are countervailing factors, such as the need for incentives, that suggest that an ideal society will not be completely equal. Nevertheless, the reasons for deviations from equality should be scrutinized closely. As we saw in Chapter 11, the great disparities of wealth and income in the United States and worldwide cannot be justified by incentives or anything else.

The inevitable conclusion derived from an afreeist perspective is that we should try to distribute more equitably the benefits of society—material benefits, but also the benefits of intangibles such as freedom. This should affect how we think about economic activity, taxes, regulation, foreign policy, immigration, foreign aid, and a host of other issues.

Part III

Personal Afreeism

Chapter 14

Principles of Afreeist Living

AFREEISM CAN GIVE US A BETTER SENSE of our place in the universe and in our world. The afreeist perspective is humbling, but it is also comforting and energizing. Ironically, afreeism can be freeing. A thoroughgoing afreeist, someone who has truly managed rationally and emotionally to shed completely the belief in free will, will also free herself of guilt, blame, regret, and remorse. She will be more humble and more resilient. Such a person will be accepting of others, not just of people of other cultures, races, religions, sexual orientations, gender identities, and appearances, but also more accepting of people who have spoken or acted in ways that she finds antisocial, offensive, or otherwise against her interests.

Part III of this book discusses the personal implications of afreeism. This involves both how we view ourselves and how we view others. As we saw with social policy, understanding that the world is deterministic and accepting that we do not have free will can lead to some profound shifts in our thinking and in how we live our lives. That said, afreeism is not a comprehensive life philosophy. It cannot be a complete roadmap to good living. It will not tell you how to find love or how to advance in your career. Rather, it is a perspective. Within that perspective there is room for numerous life philosophies and approaches. There is much to learn about life that has nothing to do with afreeism.

Learning From Others

Before we begin, we should again realize that we are not the first to understand that the universe is deterministic nor the first to seek to figure out how to live with this knowledge. Others have been down this path before us and we can learn from them. Here are some strands of thought that will help guide us as we grapple with this challenge in the chapters to come.

Stoicism

The Stoics of ancient Greece were among the first thinkers to conclude that the universe is deterministic. As we learned in Chapter 7, Zeno of Citium, the founder of Stoicism, postulated a strictly deterministic universe. Some Stoics, such as Chrysippus, believed that moral desert is compatible with determinism. We can label those Stoics as semicompatibilists. As I discussed in Chapter 6, neither compatibilism nor semicompatibilism hold up to scrutiny, so we will ignore that aspect of Stoicism. Additionally, some of the advice of the Stoics, although sensible, has nothing to do with their deterministic outlook on life. In the following chapters, we will be looking primarily at the advice that flows from these thinkers' views on determinism.

Buddhism

Siddhārtha Gautama, known as Gautama Buddha or simply as the Buddha, did not espouse a conception of free will.[106] Nor did the early Buddhist philosophers. The mission of Buddhism was to alleviate suffering and to provide a means of doing so. The question of free will did not come up until Buddhist scholars began to address it in the twentieth century, and it continues to be the subject of lively debate.

For our purposes, Buddhism views the universe as an interrelated web of cause and effect. In Buddhism this web of causation is so seamless that it is impossible to delineate between the self and the rest of the universe; there is no individuated self. While not addressing determinism directly, this view of the universe did result in some ideas that resonate with determinism and afreeism.

As with many religious traditions, some of the concepts of Buddhism require unjustified leaps of faith. For example, there is currently no evidence to support the Buddhist idea of a cycle of reincarnation. Nevertheless, because the causal nature of Buddhism resonates with afreeism, there are things we can learn from it. We will consider its relevant lessons in the following chapters.

Spinoza

The philosopher Baruch Spinoza did not believe in guilt, repentance, or pity. These flow from the passions and Spinoza recognized their senselessness in a deterministic universe. Freeing oneself of these destructive impulses is possible if one understands the nature of the universe. This is precisely what afreeism tells us.

Spinoza also believed that, because the universe is causal and because we are ourselves causes, if we want to

effect change, we should strive to increase our understanding of this universe. Furthermore, Spinoza recognized
that the causal chain of events looks different looking
backward in time and forward in time. In this book, I have
tried to capture this idea through the metaphor of the lens
of causation. (See Chapter 5.)

Stoicism, Buddhism, and the philosophy of Spinoza
approach life in ways different than afreeism (although
Spinoza comes close), but they do have elements in
common with afreeism. In the chapters that follow we will
refer to these philosophical approaches to help illuminate
the implications of afreeism.

How We Approach Life Matters

Because the universe is causal, what we do matters. Imagine
ourselves again back in Robot World. If we give our robots
knowledge, it will affect the way they act. With better
knowledge, they will act in ways that better themselves and
their robot society. This is true even though their world (like
ours) is completely deterministic.

Because what we do matters, how we approach the
world and ourselves affects our happiness. The Stoics believed that happiness or sadness does not come from things
external to us. Rather it is our reaction to externals that
determines our emotional state. Marcus Aurelius wrote:

> If any external thing causes you distress, it is not the thing
> itself that troubles you, but your own judgment about it.
> And this you have the power to eliminate now.[107]

As Stoic scholar Ward Farnsworth says:

> The Stoic claim, in other words, is that our pleasures,
> griefs, desires and fears all involve three stages rather than

two: not just an event and a reaction, but an event, then a judgment or opinion about it, and then a reaction (to the judgment or opinion). Our task is to notice the middle step, to understand its frequent irrationality, and to control it through the patient use of reason.[108]

Buddhists concur. A popular Buddhist parable, known as the parable of the two arrows, goes like this:

Buddha asked a student, "If a person is struck by an arrow, is it painful?"

The student replied, "It is."

Buddha then asked, "If the person is struck by a second arrow, is that even more painful?"

The student replied, "It is."

Buddha then explained, "In life, we cannot always control the first arrow. However, the second arrow is our reaction to the first. And with the second arrow comes the possibility of choice."[109]

Buddhists sometimes distinguish pain (the first arrow) from suffering (the second arrow). From our afreeist perspective, the Buddha is suggesting that, with the knowledge that suffering comes from our reaction to external events, we may choose (in the deterministic sense) to avoid the second arrow. We may choose to avoid suffering.

Living Without Free Will

Knowledge that the universe is deterministic, then, may result in better life choices, choices that reduce suffering and increase joy, both for ourselves and others. In the following chapters, I try to coax lessons from the afreeist worldview about personal living. I divide these thoughts into three categories:

1. **Humility**–Afreeism teaches humility. First, it teaches that we are not exempt from the laws of physics. We may be special in some ways, but we are not that special. Second, it teaches that we are just a tiny part of an immense and complex causal system. Third, because this causal web is so vast and complicated, there will inevitably be things about it that we do not understand. It counsels us to be more willing to profess ignorance. Finally, on a more personal level, afreeism teaches us that our accomplishments are not truly ours. They, like everything else, were the inevitable result of forces put into play long before we existed. We should enjoy them, but we should not get too full of ourselves.

2. **Tolerance and Self-Acceptance**–Afreeism helps us to accept others and to accept ourselves. It teaches us to forgo blame, righteous anger, and condemnation. And what applies to others, applies to ourselves. Guilt, regret, and remorse make no sense in a deterministic universe. Other emotional and social reactions—such as love, empathy, gratitude, and kindness—continue to make sense. Removing our judgmental reactions allows us a more joyful existence.

3. **Engagement and Resilience**–Afreeism teaches us that, because of the causal nature of the universe, the better we understand causes, the better we can understand and affect how the universe (or our little corner of the universe) unfolds. Determinism motivates us to do science, to look for rational explanations, to be skeptical of the metaphysical or supernatural. And it prods us to action. What we do matters. And it increases our resilience. What happened had to happen. We can accept it, learn, and move on.

None of these ideas is unique to afreeism. One can be humble, tolerant, self-accepting, engaged, and resilient even if one is not an afreeist. Yet an afreeist perspective gives these qualities a new powerful justification and salience. The afreeist perspective by its nature is humbling. It is, by its nature, tolerant. By its nature, it counsels engagement. And it makes us more resilient. Let us look at each of these virtues in turn.

Chapter 15

Humility and Wonder

THE WORLD LACKS HUMILITY. We much too often run into people who have inflated views of themselves and their accomplishments. How refreshing it is, then, to meet people who understand that their worlds are just a tiny part of the universe and who realize that their accomplishments had many contributors. From the afreeist perspective, there are four aspects of humility:

1. Humans are not exempt from the laws of nature. We may be special, but we are not that special.

2. Our lives are just a speck in time compared to the sweep of time and the immense web of causation that is the universe.

3. The web of causation is so complex and vast that we truly know little of what there is to know.

4 Our accomplishments and our failures are not ours but rather were determined to occur long before we existed.

These realizations put our lives in perspective. They help us to avoid taking ourselves so seriously. They encourage us to listen and learn, to be more willing to say "I don't know," and to be humble about our so-called accomplishments. Let's take a closer look.

The Laws of the Universe Apply to Us

Afreeism observes that the laws of nature, the laws that govern the rest of the universe, also apply to us. This may seem evident to many, but proponents of free will, most notably philosophical libertarians, argue that humans have a special faculty that allows them to be exempt from the laws of physics and causation. Yet there is strong evidence (as well as common sense) that humans are just like other physical phenomena. Indeed, no event has ever been observed that has not been the result of causes or (in the subatomic realm) randomness. True, there are some very special things about humans, in our ability to make forward-looking decisions based on reason, in our ability to communicate through language and metaphor, in our ability to adapt to our environment and engineer our environment to adapt to us. (Some of these we share with other animals.) But we are not so special that the laws of physics do not apply to us. We are not separate from the universe but part of it.

The Sweep of Time

Afreeism recognizes that the present is the result of causes (and perhaps some quantum events) that stretch back to at least the big bang, almost 14 billion years ago. The present is just a speck in time. The Stoics of ancient Greece and Rome, who were determinists, understood this. Seneca wrote:

> Imagine the vast abyss of time, and think of the entire universe; then compare what we call a human lifetime to that immensity. You will see how tiny a thing it is that we wish for and seek to prolong.[110]

And also:

> Present time is very short—so short, indeed, that for some it seems not to exist. It is always in motion, it flows and hurries on; it ceases to be before it arrives.[111]

Marcus Aurelius concurred:

> Short-lived are both the praiser and the praised, the rememberer and the remembered. And all this in just one corner of this continent—and yet even here we are not in accord with each other, nor with ourselves; and the whole of the earth, too, is a speck.[112]

Compared to the vastness of time, our very existence is short and impermanent. This can put our daily trials into perspective. Again, Marcus Aurelius:

> Think often about how quickly everything that exists, and that is coming into being, is carried away and disappears. For substance is like a river that constantly flows on: the action is constantly changing, and the causes of it operate in endless variations; almost nothing is fixed. And next to us is the boundless abyss of what has passed by and what is about to be, into which all things are lost. How then is he not a fool, who gets worked up and carried away over these things, complaining as if they were enduring and trouble-some?[113]

And again:

> You can get rid of a great number of your annoyances because they lie entirely in your own head. You will clear ample space for yourself by comprehending the scale of the universe in your mind, by observing the infinity of time, and by studying carefully the rapid change of each part of each thing—how short the time is from birth to dissolution, the time before it an abyss, the time afterwards also endless.[114]

The Stoics did not say that we should not enjoy the moment. Quite the contrary. They believed we should live in the moment. (I discuss this in Chapter 17.) Nor did they believe in inaction. They just believed that we take ourselves too seriously and that we should lighten up a bit.

Buddhism also adopts the perspective that everything about us is impermanent.

> So should you see all of the fleeting world:
> A star at dawn, a bubble in the stream
> A flash of lightning in a summer cloud;
> A flickering lamp, a phantom, and a dream.[115]

Again, this perspective should help us get through the day. The Buddha says:

> Most people never realize that all of us here shall one day perish. But those who do realize that truth settle their quarrels peacefully.[116]

Afreeism shares this perspective. The universe is a vast causal web. We occupy a tiny part of that, both in space and in time. We should act with humility. We should be prepared for change. We should understand impermanence and enjoy what have now. And when things do not go our way we should understand how little it matters. We should settle our quarrels.

The Willingness to Say "I Don't Know"

"It ain't what you don't know that gets you into trouble.
It's what you know for sure that just ain't so."
—Author Unknown[117]

The universe is deterministic. Events unfold because of a chain of causes. This does not mean that the causal chain is simple; its complexity boggles the mind. We know so little about how the universe unfolds, but science continues apace and we make progress every day. We have put a person on the moon, we have eradicated smallpox, we have created cellphones and supercomputers. Still, much remains unsolved. People continue to die of cancer, wars are common, hunger and loneliness persist. And many big philosophical questions also elude us. How did we get here? How did life begin? Does it have any purpose at all? What does it mean to live a good life?

The most appropriate answer to most of these questions is, for the present, "I don't know." Yet this seems to be a difficult admission for many, if not most. Some purport to have the answer to these questions of existence, purpose, and meaning. The earth was created in six days. Our purpose is to serve a god. Suffering is a test of faith. If we do the right things, we can attain heaven or nirvana. If we fail, then hell awaits us, or perhaps reincarnation so we might try again. So many answers, so little evidence!

Causal determinism eschews the metaphysical and the supernatural. Events are caused and, through scientific inquiry, perhaps we will learn a little about how the universe functions and where it and we are heading. Maybe we can get a bit better at making predictions. More than anything, however, the deterministic universe tells us how much we do not know. The causal web is complex and often obscure.

This applies especially to the big issues of existence, meaning, and purpose. These issues have been the subject of study and speculation throughout the centuries. It is only natural to want to know the answers. We need to continue to experiment, collect data, and ponder. We also have to accept that we may never have the answers. Causal determinism holds out hope that each day we might understand something better than we do the day before, but the enormous complexity of causal chains means that we will always have uncertainty. The humility of a simple "I don't know" is vastly better than making up "truths" that have no evidence to support them.

The Illusion of Accomplishment

In Chapter 8, in reference to afreeist social policy, I spoke of the myth of deservedness and the illusion of accomplishment. These concepts apply, perhaps with even more force, to our personal lives. In a deterministic world, our accomplishments are not truly ours but rather are the result of a chain of causation. Yes, we may be smart and creative, and we may have worked hard, but our propensity for hard work, our intelligence, and our creativity were all determined long ago.

When we look at our accomplishments, we should realize that they simply had to happen. We just happened to be the instrument. This realization should give us an abiding sense of humility. The Buddha expressed this same sentiment:

Even as a solid rock is unshaken by the wind, so are the wise unshaken by praise or blame.[118]

Afreeism tells us that accomplishment is an illusion. We should enjoy it but not become too full of ourselves. Our failures are similar. They too are the product of a chain of causation.

Understanding the deterministic nature of the universe can also mitigate what psychologists call "self-serving bias."[119] Self-serving bias is the propensity to interpret events in a way that increases our self-esteem. One manifestation of this is to take credit for whatever goes right but to blame someone else for whatever goes wrong. In the deterministic world, however, assigning blame and taking credit just do not make sense.

Even though we cannot take credit for what unfolds, we should enjoy the ride. It is like seeing a great flock of birds rise at once before a blazing sunset. We were just fortunate enough to be in the right place at the right time. The serendipity of it does not diminish our enjoyment; perhaps it even increases it.

The Wonder of It All

Learning to be humble and to accept ourselves and others removes impediments to joy. Being active in trying to improve our own lives and those of others (without the burdens of regret, remorse, or despair), can be tremendously rewarding. I believe that the afreeist perspective, besides being the most accurate representation of reality, can make life more joyful. An understanding of the deterministic universe can make us feel more connected, help us live more in the moment, encourage us to take steps to change the world for the better, and perhaps make us more appreciative and thankful for our little time upon the earth.

As we ponder the universe, it is easy to become over-come by its magnitude, complexity, and beauty. Using space telescopes such as the Hubble, scientists have found evidence of over 100 billion galaxies with hundreds of billions of stars each. Black holes, neutron stars, quasars, and other bizarre phenomena populate the universe. And at the other end of the scale, atoms, electrons, protons, neutrons, photons, quarks, neutrinos, bosons, and antimatter interact in strange non-Newtonian ways. Life itself in its dizzying variety and complexity astounds. Organisms strange and wonderful live in the most seemingly uninhabitable places, such as undersea volcanic vents and in the wind currents circling the earth.

Interdependent causal chains of immense complexity underlie all of this. We understand a small part of these chains, typically taken in isolation. The deep richness added to our lives by knowing that the universe produces such a grand tapestry and that we can experience only a bit of it for such a short time should leave us awestruck. As the late Christopher Hitchens wrote:

> This is more than enough mystery and marvel for any mammal to be getting along with.[120]

Wonder is the other side of the humility coin. Humility is the recognition of our insignificance; wonder is the appre-ciation of the magnitude, complexity, and beauty of the world around us. Stand at the edge of the Grand Canyon on a clear night with the Milky Way above like a luminous cloud. Open yourself to the vastness and beauty of the universe. It does not get any better than that.

Gratitude

Does gratitude survive determinism? If someone does something for us, is it not because it has been determined? Why should we be thankful? And what of the appreciation simply for being alive? I think of the haunting song of Mercedes Sosa:

> Gracias a la vida que me ha dado tanto
> Me dio dos luceros que cuando los abro
> Perfecto distingo lo negro del blanco
> Y en el alto cielo su fondo estrellado
> Y en las multitudes el hombre que yo amo

> Thanks to life, which has given me so much.
> It gave me two bright stars, that when I open them,
> I perfectly distinguish black from white
> And in the sky above, its starry backdrop,
> And among the multitude, the one that I love.

Whether gratitude makes sense in the deterministic universe depends on what it means to be grateful. To stand at the edge of the Grand Canyon on a starry night and feel happy you are alive is a sense of gratitude that makes sense in a deterministic world. In this connotation, we can be grateful for a beautiful sunset or a warm summer's day. Or even for winning the lottery.

Other notions of gratitude may not make sense. To feel that someone *deserves* praise for what they have done for you makes no sense. They could not have done otherwise.

This leads to the question as to whether it is ever appropriate to thank someone for what they did. Why thank someone for something that they had to do? As an example, consider a friend who has just prepared you a fine meal. The meal was excellent and the conversation scintillating. You know, however, it could not have been otherwise. Yet you are happy. In the sense above, you are happy to be alive in this moment.

You would like to convey this to your host. Why? There are several reasons why you might do so. First, as an empathetic being, you want to make your host happy. Your host is also empathetic, so knowing that you are happy will make her happy too. Second, it is informative. If your host knows what makes you happy, then she likely will invite you over again, making both of you happy. A thank-you may be the simplest way to convey the idea that what your host did brought you happiness. Unfortunately, expressing thanks can also be seen in some situations as praise, as in "She deserves to be thanked." Of course, we know that this is not true; no one deserves anything. Nevertheless, a thank-you that means that what you did made me happy, makes perfect sense in a deterministic world.

Understanding Our Place

Humility, wonder, and gratitude are all a part of understanding our place in this deterministic universe. The realization that we are subject to the laws of the universe, that we are but a small part of a vast causal web, that we know so little about this web, and that even our own accomplishments are not truly ours, all should give us both an abiding sense of humility and a feeling of wonder and gratitude. These traits should make our lives more joyful and help us bring joy to the lives of others. More on that in the next chapter.

Chapter 16

Learning Not to Blame:
Tolerance And Self-Acceptance

IN THIS LIFE, UNPLEASANT THINGS HAPPEN. People do things that hurt us or hurt other people. We do things that hurt ourselves or hurt other people. Suffering is inevitable in life. However, by understanding the deterministic universe, we mitigate much suffering. Recall the parable of the two arrows. The first arrow is the pain that the world inflicts upon us; the second is the suffering from our reaction to that pain. It comes from the guilt we feel and the blame we place on others.

In a deterministic universe it is irrational to blame others or ourselves. By understanding this, we can minimize the anger, guilt, shame, remorse, and regret. We can avoid the second arrow and live a more joyful life.

Tolerance

We tend to judge other people. Sometimes we judge people based on their actions; other times we judge people based on their intentions. We often judge people on circumstances that we know to be wholly outside of their control. For example, we might judge people because of their race, their gender, or their sexual orientation.

Afreeism emphasizes that who people are, how they act, and what intentions they have are all determined. All of us know (or should know) that this is true for things like skin color, sex, and sexual orientation. But the same is also true of actions. Because the universe is deterministic, all actions were determined long ago.

As a result, we should dispense with blame, anger, and condemnation. Without free will, people are not morally responsible for how they acted or for their intentions when they acted. Moral responsibility of this sort does not exist.

As we discussed in Chapter 10, this does not mean that people should not be punished, nor does it suggest that there should be no consequences for actions. Deterrence, for example, makes perfect sense in the deterministic world in which we live, if it is intelligently and compassionately applied. But there is no room for blame, retribution, ridicule, condemnation, righteous anger, or shaming.

But we can go further than this. Afreeism reminds us that everything is contextual. Everything is causal. Afreeism encourages us to look for reasons. Rather than blaming, we should ask, why did that person act that way? Why did she feel that way? Why did she want to do what she did? The causal universe prompts us to look for causes. Trying to figure out the causes can lead to greater understanding, which in turn can help us react better to the situation. It can also engender greater empathy. Goethe once wrote:

> With only the slightest shift in the balance of my character I believe there is no crime I could not commit.[121]

In other words: *there but for the grace of the universe go I.* All of us are driven to what we do by causal forces unleashed eons ago.

Life can be more joyful if we shed some of the anger that we have about other people, about the way they act, about their intentions, about the way that they have treated us. A Buddhist sage once analogized an angry deed with grabbing hot coals to throw at someone. It is the thrower who gets burned. A person's actions are the result of causal forces. Trying to understand these forces is the better approach. As Buddhist thinker Thich Nhat Hanh said,

> When another person makes you suffer, it is because he suffers deeply within himself, and his suffering is spilling over. He does not need punishment; he needs help. That's the message he is sending.[122]

Likewise, the determinist philosopher Spinoza wrote:

> I have striven not to laugh at human actions, not to weep at them, nor to hate them, but to understand them.[123]

Life just feels better when we treat our fellow humans as companions in life's journey, rather than as adversaries or miscreants. It feels good to stop judging.

In short, afreeism teaches that what happened, had to happen. It thereby teaches tolerance for other people, for who they are, and for how they act. It also teaches us to look for reasons for why people act as they do. Both these aspects of tolerance can only make our society work better and make us happier.

Love, Actually

In Chapter 2, I argued that love, even romantic love makes sense in a deterministic universe. A rich emotional life can contribute to our happiness. Most humans have developed a sense of empathy. Empathy, like other emotions, is a neurological phenomenon. It serves both to make us happy and to make others in our society happy. In general, we all benefit when the members of society act with empathy, kindness, and love. Understanding that the universe is deterministic does not change this. Indeed, as indicated above, understanding that the universe is deterministic removes many of the impediments to these positive emotions. We can love without debating whether someone deserves love. We can be kind without pondering whether someone deserves kindness.

Self-Acceptance

It is hard to be alive without messing up, often significantly. The more one lives, the more opportunity one has to make mistakes. We often have feelings of guilt, regret, and remorse for these actions or inactions. Feelings of guilt pervade our society. One article that appeared in the Guardian in 2017 was entitled, "Why Do We Feel So Guilty All The Time?" Its author laments:

> Filial guilt, fraternal guilt, spousal guilt, maternal guilt, peer guilt, work guilt, middle-class guilt, white guilt, liberal guilt, historical guilt, Jewish guilt: I'm guilty of them all.[124]

Guilt has been a major focus of psychological studies and theorizing at least since the time of Freud, who had a lot to say on the subject. A Google search for "scholarly articles on guilt" turns up over 2.5 million hits. Therapists routinely deal with feelings of guilt in their practices.

One of the great inventions of the Catholic Church is confession. In the Catholic Church, you can go into the confessional, confess your sins, do your penance (typically saying a handful of prayers), and then you are forgiven. You can move on with your life. And this includes the worst possible sins. Of course, not all of our errors are sins. However, for those that are sins, the sacrament of confession confers forgiveness on the sinner and can alleviate feelings of guilt, regret, and remorse.

But afreeism is even better. In our deterministic universe, guilt, regret, and remorse are irrational. Because the world is determined, we made the only decisions we could have made. How can we blame ourselves for past actions when those actions were determined? Someone who truly understands the deterministic nature of the universe should be free of guilt, regret, remorse, and self-blame. Even if you ended up where you are because of poor values, poor judgment, uncontrolled emotions, or unhealthy desires, all of these were determined by a chain of causation that began eons ago.

Pain in life is unavoidable. We sometimes hurt and we sometimes hurt other people. It is quite natural to feel pain and sadness when we see others, both loved ones and strangers, in pain. But it does not help to add regret, remorse, shame, or guilt to our pain and sadness. We should learn from the past. We should analyze the chain of causation that led to undesirable ends—doing so will help us act more wisely in the future—but we should not beat ourselves up over past choices.

An Exercise

People can be full of regret and remorse. They made the wrong career choice. They married the wrong person and stayed in the unhappy marriage for far too many years. They had an affair, which destroyed their marriage and ruined their relationship with their children. They made the wrong financial decisions. They put their money in foolish investments or they lost it gambling. They avoided going to the doctor for too long, allowing the cancer to progress. They put their kids into the wrong schools. They were absent as parents. They trusted the wrong people.

Afreeism teaches us that it makes no sense to feel regret for these actions. But regret is a powerful emotion and we have been socially programmed to feel it. How do we overcome it?

One way is through visualization. Imagine that you are a free-floating bodiless soul. (This is just an exercise; you do not have to believe in the existence of souls.) What would happen if you were randomly placed into the body of someone you did not know? (Suppose that the previous soul had to vacate the body for unknown reasons and that you are taking its place.) The body that you have come to inhabit has a history, which is now your history. What do you do?

In whatever body you have been placed, you must decide how to move forward with the new life that you have just inherited. For a start, you assess your present situation. Are you married or single, what is your financial situation, do you have children, what are your children's situations, etc. Clearly, you will have challenges. There are things from your inherited history that you will have to deal with. Perhaps the body that you inhabit committed some crime or insulted someone or had a bad relationship with her mother. There may be some stories from this history that make you smile and feel good; others might make you cringe. Others will teach you things. You might prefer that the person who formally occupied the body had not done some of the things she did, but you cannot feel any personal responsibility for them or any personal regret for having done them, because you were not even there.

In a sense, this is the situation we are in. Sure, we did some things that we wish we had not been caused to do, but we cannot regret them because they simply had to happen. We now have to assess our situation and deal with what we have going forward.

This leads to the following morning exercise. Get up, have your cup of coffee or tea and then sit quietly for a moment imagining that you have simply been put into this body and this life this very morning. No regrets, no guilt. You are not responsible for what has happened. Now assess where you are and move on.

Not only will this exercise help rid your psyche of feelings of guilt, regret, and remorse, it might also give you an appreciation for the good fortune that you have had. Of all the bodies that you could have inhabited, you somehow ended up with this one. For many of us, this is far better than most of the other bodies in the world that we could have gotten stuck in. If we have had this good fortune, then it is important to remember that this is not true for everyone. Some people have inherited histories, character traits, family situations, and health conditions far worse than ours. They are not responsible for this. Their lives were determined just as much as ours. This brings us back again to that old (modified) chestnut: *there but for the grace of the universe go I.* This should give us a bit of empathy.

Learning Not To Blame

Blame makes no sense in a deterministic world. It is also detrimental to relationships, to understanding, to acceptance, and to self-acceptance. Judging other people saps our energy and often affects our moods. Deciding not to judge can bring a sense of relief, of peace, of calm, and even of curiosity. Rather than looking to blame, we should instead look for reasons for people's actions and try to understand why they acted the way they did. We should look for the causes of their actions. And we should treat ourselves to the same consideration. We are not to blame; there is no reason to feel guilt or regret or remorse. Rather, we should accept where we are and try to learn from our experiences. Why did we do what we did? How did it work out? Can we do better next time? And then we need to move on.

Chapter 17

Engagement and Resilience

ENGAGEMENT IS OUR WILLINGNESS and commitment to get involved, to take an active part in the unfolding of the universe and participate with the beings that inhabit it. Resilience is our ability to take what the universe throws at us. Here are some aspects of engagement and resilience:

1. **Connectedness**—Being engaged is understanding that we are all linked to each other and to everything else through the complex causal web that is the universe.

2. **Presence**—Being engaged involves living in the present, not being fixated on the past or paralyzed by the future. The past is useful for learning, but we are not responsible for it. We can affect the future, but we should not be overwhelmed by it. We live in the present moment.

3. **Inquisitiveness**—Being engaged is being inquisitive. There are both aesthetic and practical sides to this. Aesthetically, the universe is so vast, so splendid in its detail and variety, so full of unexpected beauty, that it invites our curiosity. On the practical side, what we do

affects the future. To understand how best to affect the future, we need to understand as much as we can about how the world works. To engage productively with the universe, we need knowledge. What makes our world work? What makes our society function for the benefit of all? What makes our fellow humans tick?

4. **Protagonism**—Protagonism is the impetus to action, to actively taking part in and making decisions about one's own life, to being the protagonist in one's own life story. The foundation of afreeism is the understanding that the universe is causal. Because it is causal, we can affect the future. What we do matters. Afreeism invites us to act.

5. **Resilience**—Not only can we affect the universe, the universe can affect us. We are the result of forces unleashed at the beginning of time. Our world is full of beauty and pleasure. It is also full of ugliness and pain. Understanding the causal nature of the universe may help us better endure what the universe throws at us.

Let us look at each of these aspects.

Connectedness

Being part of the universe means that we are connected to it. Because of the web of causation, everything connects with, affects, and is affected by everything else. Determinism reminds us that we are not islands.

Afreeism shares this sense of connectedness with Buddhism, whose writings evidence a deterministic worldview. The Buddhist notion of causation and interdependence is often expressed as follows:

This is, because that is. This is not, because that is not. This comes to be, because that comes to be. This ceases to be, because that ceases to be.[125]

Or, put more succinctly recently by the Dalai Lama:

We Buddhists believe that the entire world is interdependent.[126]

Indeed, Buddhism holds that the world is so connected and seamless that one cannot even tell where a person ends and the rest of the universe begins. This, in Buddhism, is the denial of the self. According to Buddhism we are part of the web of the universe and there is no real boundary between the set of causes that we sometimes refer to as "me" and those that we sometimes refer to as "not me." Afreeists see the world in much the same way.

In a popular Ted Talk,[127] neuroscientist Dr. Jill Bolte Taylor describes what happened to her when a massive hemorrhage shut down the left side of her brain. The right and left sides of the brain operate quite differently. Dr. Bolte Taylor describes right-side function informed by both her empirical research and her personal experience resulting from her trauma:

Our right human hemisphere is all about this present moment. It's all about "right here, right now." . . . Information, in the form of energy, streams in simultaneously through all of our sensory systems and then it explodes into this enormous collage of what this present moment looks like, what this present moment smells like and tastes like, what it feels like and what it sounds like. I am an energy-being connected to the energy all around me through the consciousness of my right hemisphere. We are energy-beings connected to one another through the consciousness of our right hemispheres as one human family. And right here, right now, we are brothers and sisters on this planet, here to make the world a better place. And in this moment we are perfect, we are whole and we are beautiful.

The left side is quite different. It takes the present moment, decides what is important, relates it to the past and to the future. The left side has a sense of self, a sense of separateness, a sense of time.

When Dr. Bolte Taylor, lost the left side of her brain, she lost her sense of separateness:

> And then I lost my balance, and I'm propped up against the wall. And I look down at my arm and I realize that I can no longer define the boundaries of my body. I can't define where I begin and where I end, because the atoms and the molecules of my arm blended with the atoms and molecules of the wall.... But then I was immediately captivated by the magnificence of the energy around me. And because I could no longer identify the boundaries of my body, I felt enormous and expansive. I felt at one with all the energy that was, and it was beautiful there.

Of course, the simple dichotomy of left brain/right brain does not fully capture the marvelously complex architecture of the brain. Nevertheless, Dr. Bolte Taylor's experience suggests that the sense of separateness from the rest of the universe, the sense of self, is a construct of the mind. The universe is really a complex interconnected causal web.

Even if we do not accept the Buddhist denial of self, we can acknowledge that the boundary between the self and the rest of the universe is fuzzy. Who we are is not determined just by what we are inside. Rather, we swim in a sea of expectations. The expectations of others affect how we think, how we emote, and what we consider to be appropriate behavior. Have you ever moved to a new city to start a new life? A city where you know no one and no one knows you? This typically happens several times in one's lifetime and most often when one is young. I have talked to people about this experience and discovered that the over-whelming feeling most people have when they do this is one of exhilaration, the sense that anything is possible. This comes from throwing off the expectations that box us in, the social matrix that helps define who we are and how we act. It is also a reminder about how interconnected we are.

Presence

When Dr. Bolte Taylor lost the left side of her brain, she also lost the concepts of past and future, along with all the regrets about the past and worries for the future. She recounts:

> So here I am in this space, and my job, and any stress related to my job—it was gone. And I felt lighter in my body. And imagine all of the relationships in the external world and any stressors related to any of those—they were gone. And I felt this sense of peacefulness. And imagine what it would feel like to lose 37 years of emotional baggage! Oh! I felt euphoria, . . . euphoria! It was beautiful. . . . And my spirit soared free, like a great whale gliding through the sea of silent euphoria. Nirvana. I found Nirvana.

People often forget to live in the moment. They are either mired in the past, about what should have or could have been, or worried about the future. As we saw in Chapter 16, afreeism teaches us to let go of the past. Feelings of guilt, regret, remorse, and self-blame, do not make sense. Afreeists look to the past for only two things, good memories and good lessons. Other than that, we should let go.

As for the future, since we can affect it, we do need to spend some time considering it. (One cannot survive without the left brain.) What we do today will affect what happens tomorrow so we should try to make the best choices possible.

But do we have to agonize over the future? Agonizing about the future is often the result of projected regrets. That is, we are afraid that in the future we will regret the choice we are making now. We are afraid that we will be kicking ourselves. Such fears can be paralyzing.

In a deterministic universe, it does not make sense to have regrets either now or in the future. Assimilating this notion will help us make whatever decisions we need to make now and then get back to enjoying today.

The Stoics had this perspective. Here is the Roman Stoic Marcus Aurelius:

> Keep this in mind, that each of us lives only this present and indivisible moment. Everything else has either already been lived or is uncertain.[128]

The Stoics believed that most people spend too much time fixated on both the past and the future. Rather we should make the best decisions we can and then stop worrying. The past is over and the future will work out as it will. Here is Marcus Aurelius again:

> Do not disturb yourself by imagining your whole life at once. Don't always be thinking about what sufferings, and how many, might possibly befall you. Ask instead, in each present circumstance: "What is there about this that is unendurable and unbearable?" You will be embarrassed to answer.[129]

Seneca agrees:

> Memory recalls the torments of fear, and foresight antic-
> ipates them. It is only the present that makes no one
> wretched.[130]

Again, Seneca was not saying that we should ignore
either the past or the future:

> Both the future and the past can delight us—one in
> anticipation, the other in memory—but one is uncertain
> and may not happen, while the other cannot fail to have
> been. What madness it is, therefore, to lose our grip on that
> which is the surest thing of all![131]

The surest thing of all is the present. If we rest too much
of our happiness on what has been and what will be, we will
be missing out on the most important source of happiness:
that which is happening now. Seneca contemplates the consequences of not living in the now:

> Think about individuals; consider men in general; there is
> not one whose life is not focused on tomorrow. What harm
> is there in that, you ask? Infinite harm. They are not really
> living. They are about to live.[132]

He continues:

> Two things we must therefore root out: fear of distress in
> the future and the memory of distress in the past. The one
> concerns me no longer. The other concerns me not yet.[133]

The Buddha concurs:

> Let not a person revive the past
> Or on the future build his hopes
> For the past has been left behind
> And the future has not been reached
> Instead with insight, let him see
> Each presently arisen state

Let him know that and be sure of it
Invincibly and unshakably
Today the effort must be made;
Tomorrow, death may come, who knows?[134]

The modern practice of mindfulness (a practice highly influenced by Buddhism), largely adopts this perspective. Here is Thich Nhat Hanh, a Buddhist teacher of mindfulness:

Do not lose yourself in the past. Do not lose yourself in the future. Do not get caught in your anger, worries or fears, come back to the present moment, and touch life deeply. This is mindfulness.[135]

Again, worrying about the past makes no sense in a deterministic universe. The past is only valuable for good memories and lessons. As for the future, since the universe is causal and what we do matters, afreeism concludes that we must pay it some attention. But we should not worry about the future or otherwise agonize over our decisions. When we arrive there, we will realize it all had to happen.

Inquisitiveness

Afreeism emphasizes the deterministic causal nature of the universe, the idea that the universe is governed by laws, not by gods or demons. It eschews the supernatural and demands evidence. The more we understand the causes that determine the universe, the better we can shape the world and ourselves so we can live and thrive. We should be inquisitive, questioning, curious, skeptical. We should educate ourselves.

One does not have to be an afreeist to understand the power and potential of knowledge. Yet many are susceptible to making exceptions. A scientist may be rigorously scientific at work but abandon scientific skepticism and rigor at the door of her church. Likewise, a doctor may understand why a tumor causes tremors in a patient at the hospital but in the jury box may condemn a criminal to brutal imprisonment at the alter of free will. There is no shortage of examples. People parse horoscopes, employ spiritual mediums, and look to karma.

Afreeism teaches us that the universe is causal. Rather than relegate answers to priests and shamans, we need to strive for a genuine understanding of the way the world works. This applies to basic science, but it also applies to our relationships and everyday life. Rather than trying to explain the behavior of others simplistically ("she is just a bad person"), we should try to understand what caused a person to do what she did and what molded her character. A greater understanding of the universe and of people can only make our lives better.

Protagonism

Protagonism refers to the impetus to actively take part in and make decisions about our own lives. This is one of the most difficult aspects of afreeism to understand. Since we do not have free will and since everything has been determined, why should we ever concern ourselves about the future? I addressed this in Chapter 5 using the metaphor of the Lens of Causation and I will revisit this briefly here because it is such an important implication of afreeism.

Determinism is based on causation and causation implies that the future is, in part, determined by what we do. Our choices are determined; nevertheless, different choices bring different results. We are all part of the causal web of the universe and what we do ripples across that causal web. Our actions have consequences. If I stick myself with a pin, I will feel pain. So I do not do it.

Consider once more Robot World. We may observe in Robot World that the robots whose internal algorithms cause them to consider the future, to educate themselves, and to act accordingly do better than robots who take a more passive approach. Indeed, the robots themselves may notice this and may as a result adopt a more active lifestyle.

We are the same. Even though the universe is deterministic, we can notice that humans who consider the future, educate themselves, and act accordingly do better than humans who do not do these things.

This was the observation of Spinoza who, despite being a thoroughgoing determinist, had an elaborate philosophy on how to act and how to approach the world. For Spinoza, it is important to educate ourselves on the nature of the world and the mind and to act accordingly. (Spinoza's prescriptions echo those of the Stoics in examining our reactions to events rather than dwelling on the events themselves.)

Because the world is causal, what I do affects my life and the lives of others. For example, if I throw myself into social activism, perhaps I can make changes in society that improve the lot of thousands of people. As such, afreeism is a call to action and issues us a challenge to be the protagonist in our own lives. As noted before, the Stoics (our Greek determinists) were people of action. Because the universe is causal, and because we are one of the causes, we can make a difference.

Resilience

Bad things happen. Some are the result of things other people do and others result from our own actions. Still others may have no human agent. The death of a child from cancer or from a seemingly random genetic defect are examples of this. And sometimes we are just in the wrong place at the wrong time.

In Chapter 16, I wrote of tolerance and self-acceptance. Afreeism teaches us to be tolerant of other people, not just of who they are but also of what they do. Tolerance is a form of resilience. It helps us to understand and accept what other people do even if it affects us adversely. Self-acceptance is also a form of resilience. Understanding that we are not morally responsible for what we have done or for what we have become helps us to accept the past, learn from it, and move on.

Finally, unfortunate events that just happen for no apparent reason are still caused, still inevitable. Understanding that these occurrences were determined from the beginning of time may help us withstand the blow and move on.

Amor Fati

The Stoic doctrine of *amor fati* takes these ideas to another level. (The expression was coined by Nietzsche but the idea comes from the Stoics.) *Amor fati* means love of fate. It means learning to love whatever happens. We cannot change the past or even the present circumstances that we find ourselves in. To be happy, then, we need to embrace our present situation and even learn to love it no matter how challenging it might be.

An Exercise

The Stoics believed that we could better learn to accept the past, prepare for the future, and enjoy the present. They developed an exercise to help us accomplish this. The modern term for this ancient practice is negative visualization.[136] Negative visualization is the present contemplation of future loss or failure. There are several reasons to engage in this exercise. One is to enhance the enjoyment of the things we have now, to keep us from succumbing to hedonic adaptation, which occurs when we get so used to the good things in our lives that they no longer please us.

Another reason to engage in negative visualization is to help us prevent some loss or failure in the first place. Psychologist Gary Klein applied this technique in a business environment by asking managers, before a project is accepted or launched, to visualize the project failing and then to give a "premortem" on why it failed.[137] Contemplating what can go wrong, whether in business or in our personal lives, helps us to prevent a negative outcome from occurring.

The third reason to engage in negative visualization is to prepare us emotionally if the loss or failure occurs. As Seneca says,

> He robs present ills of their power who has perceived their coming beforehand.[138]

In his book on Stoic philosophy, Professor William B. Irvine writes about the Greek Stoic Epictetus along the same lines:

> [Epictetus] counsels us, for example, when we kiss our child, to remember that she is mortal and not something we own—that she has been given to us "for the present, not inseparably nor forever." His advice: In the very act of

kissing the child, we should silently reflect on the possibility that she will die tomorrow. [Epictetus, "Discourses," II.xxiv.86,88] In his Meditations, Marcus Aurelius approvingly quotes this advice. [Marcus, XI.34][139]

This negative visualization not only increases our enjoyment of our child today, it helps us protect her going forward and prepares us for what could happen tomorrow. Note that in this formulation there is both action, looking toward the future, and acceptance regarding the past. Negative visualization helps us with both.

Engagement and Resilience

Causation is the root of both engagement and resilience. Because of causation, what we do matters. We are causes; we can push the universe ever so slightly. We can make our little corner better. However, because of causation, the universe pushes back, and sometimes it pushes back harshly. We need resilience to survive those pushes and to thrive in spite of them. Understanding the causal nature of the universe helps us both to engage and to rebound.

Chapter 18

Meaning and Purpose

THIS SHORT CHAPTER is on the meaning of life and on reasons to get up in the morning. What indeed is the meaning of life, particularly in a deterministic world? Philosophers have engaged this question since the beginning of recorded history and almost certainly before that. Indeed, the search for meaning is perhaps the single most important inquiry of philosophy.

You will not find the answer to the meaning of life here. If anything, the realization that the universe is deterministic makes that question more difficult. What meaning could life possibly have if the universe unfolds deterministically, if all human actions are determined from the beginning of time? Although it doesn't provide the answer, afreeism may be able to help us clarify our thinking.

What Does Meaning Mean?

Religious thought often derives meaning and purpose from an all-powerful, all-knowing, all-good deity. In this conception, the deity creates humans (and everything else) for the deity's reasons and purposes. These reasons and purposes are not necessarily known to, or even knowable by, humans. The purpose of an individual is simply to obey (and perhaps fear or love) the deity. By obeying the deity, the person is furthering the deity's purpose, however inscrutable it may be. This obedience is purpose enough for humans, although there may be the additional benefit of a reward, such as heaven, a favorable reincarnation, or per-haps good fortune here on earth.

Note that this description addresses two notions of meaningfulness:

1. Why are we here?

2. What constitutes a meaningful life?

The theistic answers to these questions are typified by the Christian responses to these questions. We are here because God created us for his purposes. A meaningful life is one lived by the rules that God has set out for us. God's plan is what gives our life meaning. As Nietzsche recognized, again referring to Christianity, meaning requires,

> A kind of unity, some form of "monism": and as a result of this belief man becomes obsessed by a feeling of profound relativity and dependence in the presence of an All. . . . At bottom, man loses the belief in his own worth when no infinitely precious entity manifests itself through him.[140]

Other monotheistic systems, such as Judaism and Islam, have similar doctrines around meaning.

Meaning and Purpose

Belief systems do not have to be theistic to convey meaning. Buddhism, Taoism, and Confucianism all create metaphysical systems that define meaning. These systems typically skip the first question of why we exist. As to the second, these belief systems provide that a meaningful life is one that is lived according to the precepts of the system.

The above description of nontheistic systems applies broadly. Soviet communism and Nazi nationalism both were belief systems that gave their adherents purpose, defined what the good life was, and prescribed how to find meaning in life. Both had their canonical texts, their charismatic leaders, their gardens of Eden, and their demands for complete loyalty. Indeed, we can even find similar characteristics in the writings of some of the advocates of capitalism, socialism, and other economic and social systems.

These dogmatic viewpoints have advantages and disadvantages. The disadvantage is that they depend on faith—that is, on an adherence to beliefs without recourse to evidence or experimentation. One simply believes. As a result, any belief can be justified, from the benevolent to the heinous. The advantage of dogmatic viewpoints is that, since they do not have to justify their beliefs, they can describe fairly easily what is a meaningful life. A meaningful life is one led in accordance with the rules of the deity (or, in the case of nontheistic religions, with the rules of the system.)

Afreeism and Meaning

Afreeism is not *necessarily* inconsistent with a belief in a deity or a belief in a metaphysical system. Some religious traditions embrace determinism, although most do not.

However, afreeism may conflict with religious or meta-physical systems in two ways. First, if the religious or metaphysical system embraces the belief in free will, then the system is incompatible with afreeism. Second, afreeism is not faith-based. Instead, it is based on empirical observation and logical reasoning. This may make it difficult for the afreeist to embrace faith-based arguments even if they do not directly contradict afreeism.

Afreeism has contrasting advantages and disadvantages to religious belief. Afreeism does not accept things on faith. Skepticism is one of its foundational values. The rejection of free will and desert all come from the notion that the universe is causal, a conclusion borne out by evidence. In contrast, as to the question of why we are here, the afreeist response is simply that we don't know. Indeed, there does not appear to be any reason why we are here beyond the fortunate coming together of physical forces.

These same physical forces will lead to our destruction. The sun will someday become a supernova and engulf the solar system. The world will perish and so will the human race. Even if we somehow manage to escape the solar system in time, and establish a thriving society elsewhere, those suns too will supernova or collapse. Nothing lasts forever and the human race is no exception.

The realization that the universe is deterministic may further add to the skepticism as to whether life has meaning. Even if we were not doomed to oblivion, what meaning could possibly exist in a universe where every action, every thought, every gesture, is determined by causal factors in place since the beginning of time?

Nietzsche claimed that the main function of religion was to give meaning to life. When religion dies, so does meaning. This was, according to Nietzsche, what was happening in Europe:

Meaning and Purpose

At bottom, man has lost the faith in his own value when no infinitely valuable whole works through him; i.e., he conceived such a whole in order to be able to believe in his own value.[141]

In Europe, where Nietzsche was writing, this "infinitely valuable whole" was Christianity. "God is Dead," Nietzsche had previously observed, leading him to conclude: "Nihilism stands at the door . . ."[142]

Beyond this observation, Nietzsche had no answers (or at least none that he was willing to commit to pen and paper) for the possibility that there was no meaning at all. Hence the descent into nihilism.

Perhaps afreeism is another nail in the coffin of meaning. Perhaps not. Before considering whether one can live a meaningful life in a deterministic universe, let us recognize that nihilism does have some redeeming features. The fall of a universal Christian conception in the West of what is a good and meaningful life opened up the world for those living outside the contours of the Christian ideal. As philosopher Sean Kelly has written:

. . . when the structure of a worthwhile and well-lived life is no longer agreed upon and taken for granted, then a new sense of freedom may open up. Ways of living life that had earlier been marginalized or demonized may now achieve recognition or even be held up and celebrated. Social mobility—for African Americans, gays, women, workers, people with disabilities or others who had been held down by the traditional culture—may finally become a possibility.[143]

But there is a downside. In the same article, Kelly remarks:

Without any clear and agreed upon sense for what to be aiming at in a life, people may experience the paralyzing type of indecision depicted by T.S. Eliot in his famously vacillating character Prufrock; or they may feel, like the characters in a Samuel Beckett play, as though they are continuously waiting for something to become clear in their lives before they can get on with living them; or they may feel the kind of "stomach level sadness" that David Foster Wallace described, a sadness that drives them to distract themselves by any number of entertainments, addictions, competitions, or arbitrary goals, each of which leaves them feeling emptier than the last.[144]

Without a faith-based metaphysical system that proclaims what a meaningful life is, and facing the fact of a universe governed by determinism, the afreeist must confront the problem of nihilism.

Meaning in a Deterministic World

Afreeism rejects dogmatic assertions of meaning yet offers no simple answer to the challenge of nihilism. Perhaps we will simply have to learn to live without the sort of unifying meaning that religious dogmas provide. That said, we can take a few moments to speculate about whether, in a deterministic world, life can have any meaning and whether it is possible to live with purpose.

First, as to the question of why we are here, afreeism counsels humility. We just do not know. There is likely no reason at all and, if there is a reason, we are likely never to know it. This does not mean that we should not look for reasons. It just means that we should not create reasons where none are apparent.

What about the second, perhaps more important, question: what is it to lead a meaningful life? Of course, this question is not unique to afreeism. Anyone who has overthrown dogma, anyone who lives her life through inquiry and skepticism, must face this question. The fact that afreeists recognize the deterministic nature of the universe changes nothing in this regard.

Since the problem of meaning is one afreeists share with atheists and agnostics, we can perhaps get some insight from how these non-believers approach this problem. Interestingly, empirical evidence suggests that atheists do not have any more difficulty in finding meaning in life than do religious adherents. A recent study of data involving 1200 subjects found that atheists and the religiously unaffiliated are no more nihilistic than religious adherents. They all found meaning in roughly equal percentages. Where they found meaning, however, differed significantly. The religiously affiliated found their meaning in external sources whereas for atheists and the religiously-unaffiliated meaning was self-produced.[145]

Of course, atheists are not necessarily afreeists. The determinism of afreeism may create additional challenges to the discovery or creation of meaning. Nevertheless, the case of atheism is instructive. And, once more, we can harken back to the deterministic stoic philosophers of ancient Greece and Rome who led active purpose-driven lives.

The Source of Meaning

So here are some thoughts on meaning and whence it comes. Through biological and social evolution, we have developed into beings that are highly social and highly interdependent. As such, some activities give us pleasure as individuals, and others give us pleasure as social animals. Some pleasures are simple and atavistic, such as the pleasure of having sex or having a great meal. Others are perhaps more complex, such as the pleasure of a good relationship, an intriguing conversation, or a friendly competition.

Not all of our pleasures are good for us or good for society. We may overeat, drink too much, or overindulge in recreational drugs. At times, we may find pleasure in harming those we do not like or in expropriating their goods. To counteract some of these anti-social pleasures, social and biological evolution favored us with empathy. Empathy cannot eliminate all of our negative social tendencies so we developed institutions to pick up the slack. We have laws and other mechanisms for enforcing social norms. And we can reason. Through these mechanisms we have learned to curb many of our negative impulses. The process of social evolution continues. For example, I have suggested in this book that through reason we can overcome our natural tendency towards vindictiveness and retribution.

All of our pleasures, the good and the bad, are at base neurological phenomena. Our brains have developed in certain ways, through the operation of both biological and social evolution, to enjoy certain things and to dislike others.

To the afreeist meaning is just another neurological phenomenon formed through biological and social evolutionary processes. The feeling that one's life has meaning or purpose comes from a particular configuration in the brain. This is not to diminish its significance. Empirically, people report that having a meaningful or purpose-driven life is immensely satisfying.

In this book, I have identified a number of neurological phenomena. These phenomena are the result of biological and social evolution. Some of these, I have suggested, we as humans and as members of society have outgrown. I have gone so far as to say that some of these now hinder our development as a society and our happiness as members of that society. These include the belief in free will, the propensity to blame, the desire to exact retribution, and the belief in worthiness. Other phenomena function to make our lives better. These include love, humility, tolerance, self-acceptance, and empathy.

Meaningfulness is one of those neurological phenomena that makes our lives better and more joyful. On the personal level, meaningfulness is tied to individual survival and thriving. We find meaning in developing ourselves to our fullest potential. But meaningfulness also has a social aspect, tied to the survival of society. It benefits society and its members when we develop strong social bonds with each other and also when we think and act outside of ourselves for the benefit of society. Put another way, we have evolved to care about and internalize the larger concerns of society. We have evolved to find meaning in actions that benefit others. We have evolved to be empathetic.

This does not answer the question for any particular person as to what sorts of things will bring meaning to that person's life. It does suggest some possible directions, however. Looking to both the personal and social aspects of meaning, we can identify some likely avenues of exploration. Here are some possible aspects of a meaningful life:

1. Personal development: Advancing ourselves to our fullest potential.

2. Social engagement: Interacting with family, friends, and society.

3. Other-directed purpose: Finding or creating a purpose outside of ourselves.

This is not a prescription; each individual must find meaning on her own terms. Particularly as to other-directed purposes, afreeism offers very little guidance as to what one's purpose should be. Perhaps one's other-directed purpose is simply providing for one's family. Perhaps it is writing a great novel. Perhaps it is working in the healing arts or helping people with their plumbing. Sometimes the answer to the question of what should be my other-directed purpose is found by simply picking something, doing it, and then evaluating the satisfaction you derive from it.

In all, I believe that these three aspects of meaning encompass the things that get us out of bed in the morning. These are what make life worth living. Naturally, these observations are not unique to afreeism.

One final observation. One other-directed purpose is working directly towards a better society, towards better social policies. This could include working within an NGO, advocating in the workplace, or even working on a political campaign. Afreeism cannot define with great specificity what a good society is, but as we have seen, it does offer some guidance. The Equality Principle introduced in Chapter 8 flows directly from the afreeist observation that nothing is ever deserved. Afreeist ideas support a more humane criminal justice system, a more just economic system, and a more humane and fair immigration system. These ideas and others can be cobbled together to create a vision of a good society, perhaps even an inspiring one. Working towards these goals can contribute to a meaningful life.

Of course, the choices we make in this regard (and all others) have all been determined. If we are fortunate, our decision-making algorithm will incorporate the notions of a meaningful life. We will seek self-fulfillment, deep personal relationships, and other-directed purpose. An afreeist can embrace these aspects of meaning without contradiction.

Conclusion

IN THIS BOOK, I PRESENTED one fundamental idea: we have no free will. I called the disbelief in free will *afreeism*. It is an idea based in science and reason, requiring no leaps of faith. It is an idea whose origins date back over two millennia, and at the same time is bolstered by modern scientific discovery.

The most important ideas in this book, however, are those related to the *implications* of abandoning the belief in free will. Abandoning free will radically alters the way we see the world. It changes how we view and treat one another. It shakes up our conceptions of the good society and of good social policy. It has the potential to make us better people, to remove impediments to our own happiness, and to increase the joy we find in life.

The Stoics, the Buddhists, and a number of prominent philosophers understood this. Without free will, there can be no moral responsibility for past actions. Without moral responsibility, there should be no regret, remorse, guilt, or shame, and no retribution. The criminal justice system continues to function, but in an altered, more humane way. We treat each other with more tolerance and compassion; we treat *ourselves* with more tolerance and compassion. Life becomes more joyful.

These ideas represent a rough guide for living. They are my reflections and those of the thinkers from earlier eras we met in these pages on whose shoulders I stand. As a guide for living, these ideas are not authoritative, but rather tentative. They are the beginning of an inquiry and perhaps of a conversation. Afreeism does not answer all of the questions of life. Far from it. Rather it is a framework for looking at and interacting with the world. I hope that you have found these ideas interesting, provocative, and worthy of discussion. But, most of all, I hope that you will find them useful.

For more information on the ideas and ideals of afreeism, please visit the Afreeist Society website at afreeism.org.

Endnotes

[1] Sapolsky (2017) 33.

[2] Harari, Yuval Noah. Sapiens (pp. 305-306). Harper. Kindle Edition

[3] *Letter to Menoeceus*, 134.

[4] Harris (2012), 11-12.

[5] Kestembaun (2018).

[6] See Sapolsky (2017) 79.

[7] Saunders (2017).

[8] Turing (1950).

[9] This is an old proverb. There are versions going back at least to the 1200s. Benjamin Franklin included a version in his Poor Richard's Almanack. The version quoted here comes from James Baldwin (1912).

[10] "Another signature of dynamical chaos is aperiodic motion that is generally so complex as to resemble a random process. Yet the process is not random: ... it is still governed by "implacable natural laws"—there is an underlying order implied by the fact that the paths followed by the system's constituents are the solution of a perfectly well-defined set of deterministic differential equations of motion. . . . "Chaos," in its present usage, means deterministic chaos. The terms "random," "stochastic," "noisy" are descriptive of another class of phenomena associated with probabilistic theories where chance enters the picture, as in statistical mechanics and quantum theory. Regrettably, stochastic behavior and deterministic chaos are all too readily confused in popular conceptualizations of chaos theory. However, they are logically distinct and, in practice, distinguishable ... (Clark 239; emphasis in the original)"

11 Everett (1957) 454-462. See also Lev Vaidman.

12 Shepherd (2016) 423.

13 Shakespeare, *Macbeth*, Act V, Scene 5.

14 The parental versions of the rule are not exactly the same as the philosophers' version. For example, Kant's categorical imperative is not consequentialist whereas the parental version appears so.

15 Rawls (1971).

16 Fischer et al. (2007) 86. See also the Stanford Encyclopedia of Philosophy (https://plato.stanford.edu/entries/freewill/) which states "An agent S is morally accountable for performing an action φ [if] S deserves praise if φ goes beyond what can be reasonably expected of S and S deserves blame if φ is morally wrong."

17 See, for example, Stent (2001), 97.

18 Frost (2019, Originally Published in 1916).

19 Irving (2009) 104.

20 A good starting point for those interested in philosophical libertarianism is Kane (2007).

21 Griffith (2013).

22 See, for example, Vargas (2007).

23 See, for example, Vihvelin (2004).

24 Dennett (1984)

25 Satel and Lilienfeld (2013) 141.

26 Satel and Lilienfeld (2013) 146.

27 See also Fischer (2007).

28 Smilanksy (2017).

29 Smilanksy (2017) attributes this idea to Strawson 2003 [originally 1961].

30 Kim and Hinds (2006).

Endnotes

[31] The philosopher Derk Pereboom (1995, 2001, 2002a, 2002b, 2009, 2012, 2013, 2014) has been a forceful proponent of this view.

[32] Dennet (2015).

[33] Caspar et al. (2017)

[34] Fischer et al. (2007) 87.

[35] Stent (2002) 109.

[36] Leucippus, Fragment 569, from Fr. 2 Actius I, 25, 4, found in Taylor (2010).

[37] See O'Conner and Franklin (2018)

[38] Derk Pereboom takes this view. See Pereboom (2009-2).

[39] Epicurus (2009, orig. date unknown).

[40] Cited in Salles (2005).

[41] Cicero, On divination 1.125, 6, trans. in Long and Sedley (1987), 55L.

[42] Evans (1968), 209.

[43] De dono perseverantiae 14.35. cited by Wetzel (2001).

[44] Mishneh Torah, Laws of Teshuvah, 5: 4 cited by Freeman (2018).

[45] Stcnt (2002) 53.

[46] http://www.jewishencyclopedia.com/articles/6337-free-will.

[47] http://www.jewishencyclopedia.com/articles/6337-free-will.

[48] http://www.jewishencyclopedia.com/articles/6337-free-will.

[49] http://www.jewishencyclopedia.com/articles/6337-free-will.

[50] Stent (2002) 49-50.

[51] Stent (2002) 53.

[52] Goodman (2009).

[53] Stent (2002), 105-106.

[54] Of Liberty and Necessity, 1654, § 11, cited in Chappell (1999).

[55] See Robinson (2017)

[56] Nadler (2019)

[57] Spinoza (1677 [2014]) Part I, Proposition XXIX

[58] Spinoza (1677 [2014]) Part I, Proposition XXVII, Corollary 2, Note.

[59] Spinoza (1677 [2014]) Part I, Appendix (Second Paragraph).

[60] See Spinoza (1670 [2001]).

[61] Rickless (2016).

[62] Goldman and Kluz (2015), 17.

[63] Laplace (1812/ trans. 1902) as quoted in Koznjak (2015), 42.

[64] Koznjak (2015).

[65] Collins (2016) Kindle Edition, Chapter 5, Location 1066.

[66] Baumeister, Masicampo, and DeWall (2009) (Abstract).

[67] Vohs and Schooler (2008).

[68] Baumeister, Masicampo, and DeWall (2009) (Abstract).

[69] Caspar et al. (2017).

[70] Caspar et al. (2017).

[71] Caspar et al. (2017).

[72] Empathy does have its limitations, however. See, for example, Bloom (2016) and Sapolsky (2017), Chapter 14, "Feeling Someone's Pain, Understanding Someone's Pain, Alleviating Someone's Pain."

[73] Sapolsky (2017), 519.

[74] Tolstoy (1869, translation 2007) 105.

[75] U. S. v. Grayson, 438 U.S. 41 (1978).

[76] Dostoevsky (1880)

[77] Hoffman (2014) 1.

Endnotes

[78] Hoffman (2014) 1.

[79] Hoffman (2014) 8.

[80] Bradley (2003) 23.

[81] Sapolsky (2017), 609-610. The dlPFC is the dorsolateral prefrontal cortex. The vmPFC is the ventromedial prefrontal cortex.

[82] For a succinct discussion of some of these programs and their effects, see Martinez (2016), 38-42.

[83] Posner (1996), 216 as reported in Martinez (2016), p. 35.

[84] Note that there are those who do not believe that deterrence is very effective. Philosopher and writer Raoul Martinez, for example, forcefully argues against the use of deterrence as a justification for punishment. Indeed, many of our notions about the effectiveness of deterrence are not supported by data.

[85] This contractualist argument for free will has been described by Smilanksy (2017) 141, which he attributes to Scanlon (1998), Scanlon (2008), Lenman (2006), Hart (1970), Honore (1999) and Gardner (2007).

[86] Weinberg (1999).

[87] http://www.prisonstudies.org/sites/default/files/resources/downloads/wppl_10.pdf. The rates for England, France, Germany, Spain are 148, 98, 79, and 147 per 100,000 respectively.

[88] See https://eji.org/mass-incarceration/prison-conditions.

[89] Sapolsky (2017), 609-610. The dlPFC is the dorsolateral prefrontal cortex. The vmPFC is the ventromedial prefrontal cortex.

[90] Isisdore (2013).

[91] USDA (2019)

[92] Collins and Hoxie (2017), 2.

[93] Collins and Hoxie (2017), 2.

[94] Saez and Zucman (2016), Table I, 552.

[95] Tax Policy Center (2016).

96 See Wolff (2017), Table 6, p. 56.

97 Bloomberg (2021)

98 Franck (2020).

99 USDA (2018).

100 Penney (2019).

101 Berlin (1969) 122.

102 BBC (2011).

103 Becchettia, et al. (2010)

104 Grullón Paz (2019).

105 Dunn (2010).

106 Repetti (2017).

107 Marcus Aurelius, *Meditations,* 8.47 (In Farnsworth (2018) [Kindle Edition, Chapter 1, Location 436.])

108 Farnsworth (2018) [Kindle Edition, Chapter 1, Location 442.])

109 This passage is cited in numerous places. I took this formulation from https://cynthiaphelps.com/dont-shoot-the-second-arrow/. Also, see https://www.dhammatalks.org/suttas/SN/SN36_6.html (English translations of suttas from the Pāli Canon.)

110 Seneca, Epistles 99.10 (In Farnsworth (2018) [Kindle Edition, Chapter 8, Location 1099.])

111 Seneca, On the Shortness of Life 10.6 (In Farnsworth (2018) [Kindle Edition, Chapter 8, Location 2839.])

112 Marcus Aurelius, Meditations 8.216 (In Farnsworth (2018) [Kindle Edition, Chapter 3, Location 1114.])

113 Marcus Aurelius, Meditations 5.23 6 (In Farnsworth (2018) [Kindle Edition, Chapter 3, Location 1128.])

114 Marcus Aurelius, Meditations 9.32 (In Farnsworth (2018) [Kindle Edition, Chapter 3, Location 1093.])

Endnotes

[115] From the Diamond Sutra. See https://www.buddhistinquiry.org/article/ three-views-of-transience/ (Barre Center for Buddhist studies.)

[116] Dhammapada, Verse 4 in Kaviratna (1980).

[117] This has been attributed to various authors including Mark Twain and Will Rogers, among others. The authorship remains in doubt.

[118] Dhammapada, Verse 81 in Kaviratna (1980).

[119] Myers (2017).

[120] Hitchens (2007).

[121] States (1987), 552.

[122] https://thichnhathanhquotecollective.com/2021/02/14/6130/ (Thich Nhat Hanh Quote Collective).

[123] Tractatus Politicus (1677) ch. 1, sect. 4. From the Oxford Reference, https://www.oxfordreference.com/view/10.1093/acref/9780191843730.001.0001/q-oro-ed5-00010359

[124] Baum (2017) 1.

[125] See https://encyclopediaofbuddhism.org/wiki/Pratiyasamutpada (Encyclopedia of Buddhism). Also, see https://www.encyclopedia.com/environment/encyclopedias-almanacs-tran scripts-and-maps/pratitya-samutpada#:~:text=The%20uniform %20and%20universal%20principle,%C4%81ya%201.262%E2%80%93264) (Enclyclopedia.com).

[126] See https://www.nationalheraldindia.com/international/dalai-lama-prayer-not-enough-to-fight-coronavirus-help-those-affected-by-it (National Herald, April 15 2020). Also, https://tibetanbuddhistsociety.org/his-holiness-the-dalai-lama-pandemic-perspective/ (Tibetan Buddhist Society, October 12, 2020).

[127] https://www.ted.com/talks/jill_bolte_taylor_my_stroke_of_i nsight/transcript?language=en#t-1018354

[128] Marcus Aurelius, Meditations 3.10 (In Farnsworth (2018) [Kindle Edition, Chapter 8, Location 2839.])

129 Marcus Aurelius, Meditations 8.36 (In Farnsworth (2018) [Kindle Edition, Chapter 8, Location 2846.])

130 Seneca, Epistles 5.9 (In Farnsworth (2018) [Kindle Edition, Chapter 8, Location 2853.])

131 Seneca, Epistles 99.5 (In Farnsworth (2018) [Kindle Edition, Chapter 8, Location 2887.])

132 Seneca, Epistles 45.12-13 (In Farnsworth (2018) [Kindle Edition, Chapter 8, Location 2860.])

133 Seneca, Epistles 78.14. (In Farnsworth (2018) [Kindle Edition, Chapter 8, Location 2887.])

134 Bhaddekaratta Sutta (2013).

135 https://thichnhathanhquotecollective.com/2018/10/23/this-is-mind-fulness/ (Thich Nhat Hanh Quote Collective).

136 See Irvine (2009) Chapter 4 for a discussion of negative visualization in Stoic philosophy.

137 Klein (2007).

138 Seneca, "To Marcia," IX:5 in Irving (2009) 65.

139 Irvine (2009) 69.

140 Nietzsche (1914).

141 Nietzsche (1914).

142 Nietzsche (1914).

143 Kelly (2010) 2.

144 Kelly (2010) 2.

145 Speed, et. al. (2018)

Bibliography

Allen et al. (2017) – J.-M. A. Allen, J. Barrett, D. C. Horsman, C. M. Lee, and R. W. Spekkens, "Quantum Common Causes and Quantum Causal Models," Phys. Rev. X 7, 031021 (2017) referenced and explained in Jacques Piennar, "Viewpoint: Causality in the Quantum World, Physics (31 July 2017 Physics 10, 86) available online at physics.aps.org/articles/ pdf/10.1103/Physics.10.86

Aurelius (cir. 170-180) – Marcus Aurelius, Meditations, translated by George Long, (Mount Vernon, New York: Peter Pauper Press, publication date unknown, probably 1940-1957).

Baldwin (1912) – James Baldwin, "The Horseshoe Nails," Fifty Famous People, available online at http://www .gutenberg.org/cache/epub/6168/pg6168-images.html.

Bhaddekaratta Sutta (2013) – Venerable U. Dhammajīva Mahā Thero, *Bhaddekaratta Sutta*, Vipassanā Fellowship, available at http://www.vipassana.com/resources/box/ dhammajiva-bhaddekarrata-vf10.pdf.

Baum (2017) – Deborah Baum, "Why do we feel so guilty all the time?" *The Guardian,* (October 3, 2017 modified February 14, 2018) available at https://www.theguard ian.com/news/2017/oct/03/why-do-we-feel-so-guilty-all-the-time

Baumeister, Masicampo, and DeWall (2009) – R. F. Baumeister, E. J. Masicampo, C. N. DeWall, "Prosocial benefits of feeling free: disbelief in free will increases aggression and reduces helpfulness." 35 *Pers. Soc. Psychol. Bull.* 35 260–268. (Abstract)

BBC (2011) – "Rwanda: How the Genocide Happened," British Broadcasting Corporation, May 17, 2011l. Available online at https://www.bbc.com/news/world-africa-13431486.

Becchettia, et al. (2010) – Leonardo Becchettia, Fiammetta Rossettia, and Stefano Castriotab "Real household income and attitude toward immigrants: an empirical analysis," The Journal of Socio-Economics, Volume 39, Issue 1, January 2010, Pages 81-88.

Berlin (1969) – Isaiah Berlin, Four Essays on Liberty (Oxford, UK: Oxford University Press, 1969).

Bloom (2016) – Paul Bloom, Against Empathy: The Case for Rational Compassion (New York: HarperCollins Publishers, 2016).

Bradley (2003) – "Retribution: The Central Aim of Punishment," 27 Harvard Journal of Law and Public Policy 19-31 (2003).

Buffet (2011) – Warren Buffet, "Stop Coddling the Super-Rich," New York Times, August 14, 2011. Available online at https://www.nytimes.com/2011/08/15/opinion/stop-coddling-the-super-rich.html?_r=0

Caspar et al. (2017) – EA Caspar, L Vuillaume , PA Magalhães De Saldanha da Gama, and A Cleeremans , "The Influence of (Dis)belief in Free Will on Immoral Behavior, " Front. Psychol. 8:20, January 13, 2017, available at https://app.dimensions.ai/details/publica tion/pub.1027676521?and_facet_journal=jour.1051810#r eadcube-epdf

Chappel (1999) – Vere Chappell, Hobbes and Bramhall on Liberty and Necessity, (Cambridge, UK: Cambridge University Press, 1999).

Collins (2016) – Chuck Collins, Born on Third Base, (White River Junction, VT: Chelsea Green Publishing, 2016).

Collins and Hoxie (2017), 2 — Chuck Collins and Josh Hoxie, "Billionaire Bonanza: The Forbes 400 and the Rest of Us" (Washington, DC: Inequality.org, Institute for Policy Studies), Nov. 2017), available at https://inequality.org/ wp-content/uploads/2017/11/BILLIONAIRE-BONANZA-2017-Embargoed.pdf.

Cornman et al. (1992) – James W. Cornman, Keith Lehrer, and George S. Pappas, Philosphical Problems and Arguments: An Introduction, 4th ed., (1992) Hacket Publishing Company, p. 95., I

Dennett (1984, 2015) – Daniel Dennett, Elbow Room, The MIT Press, 1984 (New Edition 2015).

Dostoevsky (1880) – Feodor Dostoevsky, The Brothers Ka-ramozov, "The Grand Inquisitor," (Translation by H.P. Blavatsky) The Gutenberg Project, https://www.guten berg.org/files/8578/8578-h/8578-h.htm (posted 2010).

Dunn (2010) – Kathleen Dunn, "Biological Determinism and LGBT Tolerance: A Quantitative Exploration of Bio-political Beliefs," Journal of Black Studies, 34(3):367-379, September 2010.

Epicurus (2009, orig. date unknown) – Epicurus, "Letter to Menoeceus," from Daniel C. Stevenson, The Internet Classics Archive, (Cambridge, MA: MIT, 2009), http://classics.mit.edu/Epicurus/menoec.html.

Evans (1968) – Evans, B., (ed.), Dictionary of Quotations, Delacorte Press, New York, 1968, p. 209 cited in Augustine, The Manichaean and the Problem of Evil by Hector M. Scerri.

Everett (1957) – Hugh Everett, "Relative State Formulation of Quantum Mechanics," Reviews of Modern Physics, vol. 29, No. 3, 1957.

Farnsworth (2018), Ward Farnsworth, The Practicing Stoic: A Philosophical User's Manual. (Boston: David R. Godine, Publisher, 2018).

Fischer (2007) – John Martin Fischer, "Compatibilism," in John Martin Fischer, Robert Kane, Derk Pereboom, and Manuel Vargas, Four Views on Free Will (Great Debates in Philosophy) (Malden, MA: Blackwell Publishing, 2007) 44-84.

Fischer et al. (2007) – John Martin Fischer, Robert Kane, Derk Pereboom, and Manuel Vargas, Four Views on Free Will (Great Debates in Philosophy) (Malden, MA: Blackwell Publishing, 2007).

Fontenot, Semega, and Kollar (2018) – Kayla Fontenot, Jessica Semega, and Melissa Kollar, "Income and Poverty in the United States: 2017," (Sept. 2018), United States Census Bureau, available at 11 https://www.census.gov/content/dam/Census/library/publications/2018/demo/p60-263.pdf.

Bibliography

Freeman (2018?) – Tzvi Freeman, "Free Will In Judaism," available at https://www.chabad.org/library/article_cdo/aid/3909393/jewish/Free=Will.htm#footnote17a3909393

Frost (2019, Originally Published in 1916) – Robert Frost, Road Not Taken, Cider Mill PR Book Pub LL, 2019.

Gardner (2007) – J. Gardner, Offenses and Defenses, (Oxford, UK: Oxford University Press, 2007).

Goldenbaum and Kluz (2015) – Ursula Goldenbaum and Christopher Kluz (eds.), Doing without Free Will: Spinoza and Contemporary Moral Problems (Lanham, Maryland: Lexington Books, 2015) (Adobe Digital Editions).

Goodman (2009) – Charles Goodman "Buddhism on Moral Responsibility," Consequences of Compassion: An Interpretation and Defense of Buddhist Ethics (Oxford, UK: Oxford University Press, 2009).

Griffith (2013) – Meghan Griffith, Free Will: The Basics, (New York: Routledge, 2013).

Grullón Paz (2019) – Isabella Grullón Paz, "Julián Castro on Immigration," New York Times," June 26, 2019. Available online at: https://www.nytimes.com/2019/06/26/us/politics/julian-castro-immigration.html.

Guinden (2017) – https://forward.com/scribe/377390/spinoza-s-radical-views-on-freedom-still-have-something-to-teach-us-350-yea/

Haidt and Joseph (2004) – Jonathan Haidt and Craig Joseph, "Intuitive Ethics: How Innately Prepared Intuitions Generate Culturally Variable Virtues," Daedalus: On Human Nature, 133, no. 4 (2004).

Harris (2012) – Sam Harris, Free Will (New York: Free Press, 2012).

Hart (1970) – H.L.A. Hart, Punishment and Responsibility, (Oxford, UK: Clarendon Press, 1970).

Hitchens (2007) – God Is Not Great (New York: Twelve Books, 2007.)

Hoffman (2014) – Morris B. Hoffman, The Punisher's Brain: The Evolution of Judge and Jury (Cambridge, England: Cambridge University Press, 2014).

Honore (1999) – Responsibility and Fault (Oxford UK: Hart Publishing, 1999).

Irvine (2009) – William B. Irvine, A Guide to the Good Life: The Ancient Art of Stoic Joy, (Oxford, UK: Oxford University Press, 2009).

Isidore (2013) – Chris Isidore, "Buffet says he's still paying lower tax rate than his secretary," CNN Money, (Mar. 4, 2013 10:10 AM EST), https://money.cnn.com/2013/03/04/news/economy/buffett-secretary-taxes/index.html.

Jacquet (2015) – Jennifer Jacquet, Is Shame Necessary? (New York, Pantheon, 2015).

Kahneman, Diener, Schwarz (2003) – Daniel Kahneman, Edward Diener, Norbert Schwarz, Well-Being: Foundations of Hedonic Psychology, (New York: Russell Sage Foundation, 2003).

Kane (2002) – Robert Kane (ed.), The Oxford Handbook of Free Will (New York: Oxford University Press, 2002)

Bibliography

Kane (2007) – Robert Kane, "Libertarianism," in John Martin Fischer, Robert Kane, Derk Pereboom, and Manuel Vargas, Four Views on Free Will (Great Debates in Philosophy) (Malden, MA: Blackwell Publishing, 2007) 5-43.

Katchadourian (2011) – Herant Katchadourian, Guilt: The Bite of Conscience, (Palo Alto, CA: Stanford General Books, 2011).

Kaviratna (1980) – Harischandra Kaviratna (translator), Dhammapada, Wisdom of the Buddha, (Theosophical University Press Online Edition, 1980), https://www.theo society.org/pasadena/dhamma/dham-hp.htm.

Kelly (2010) – Sean D. Kelly, "Navigating Past Nihilism," New York Times, Opinionator, December 5, 2010, available at https://opinionator.blogs.nytimes.com/2010 /12/05/navigating-past-nihilism/.

Kestembaun (2018) – David Kestembaun, "Where There is a Will: Life is a Coin With One Side," This American Life, episode 662, 16 Nov. 2018, https://www.thisamericanlife. org/662/where-there-is-a-will.

Kim, T., & Hinds, P. J. (2006). Who should I blame? Effects of autonomy and transparency on attributions in human-robot interaction. In Proceedings of RO-MAN'06. Available at http://web.stanford.edu/~phinds /PDFs/Kim-Hinds-ROMAN.pdf.

Klein (2007) – Gary Klein, "Performing a Project Pre-mortem," Harvard Business Review, (Cambridge, MA: Harvard Business School, November 2007). Available at https://hbr.org/2007/09/performing-a-project-premor tem.

Koznjak (2015) – Boris Koznak, "Who let the demon out? Laplace and Boscovich on determinism," *Studies in History and Philosophy of Science,* Part A, Volume 51, June 2015, 42-52

Kroll and Dolan (2018) – Luisa Kroll and Kerry A. Dolan (eds.), "The Forbes 400: The Definitive Ranking Of The Wealthiest Americans," Forbes Online, Oct. 3, 2018, https://www.forbes.com/forbes-400/#214ea6337e2f.

Laplace (1812/ trans. 1902) – P.S. Laplace, A philosophical essay on probabilities (F. W. Truscott & F. L. Emory, Trans.) (London: John Wiley & Sons, originally published in 1814, this translation in 1902.)

Long and Sedley (1987) - The Hellenistic Philosophers: Translations of the Principal Sources with Philosophical Commentary (Two Volumes), (Cambridge, UK: Cambridge University Press, 1987).

MacAskill (2015) – William MacAskill, Doing Good Better: How Effective Altruism Can Help You Make a Difference (New York: Avery, 2015).

Maloney (2019) – Tom Maloney, "The Best-Paid Hedge Fund Managers Made $7.7 Billion in 2018," Bloomberg Online, February 15, 2019, https://www.bloomberg.com /news/articles/2019-02-15/the-10-best-paid-hedge-fund-managers-made-7-7-billion-in-2018.

Martinez (2016) – Raoul Martinez. Creating Freedom: The Lottery of Birth, the Illusion of Consent, and the Fight for Our Future, (New York: Pantheon Books, 2016) Kindle Edition.

Bibliography

Myers (2017) – David Myers, Exploring Social Psychology, Eighth Edition, Paperback (New York: McGraw-Hill Education, 2017).

Nadler (2019) – Nadler, Steven, "Baruch Spinoza", *The Stanford Encyclopedia of Philosophy* (Spring 2019 Edition), Edward N. Zalta (ed.), https://plato.stanford.edu/archives/spr2019/entries/spinoza/

Nietzsche (1914) – Friedrich Nietzsche, The Will to Power: An Attempted Transvaluation of All Values, Volume I, Book I. Translated into English by Anthony M Ludovici in 1910. Available at https://www.gutenberg.org/files/52914/52914-h/52914-h.htm.

O'Conner and Franklin (2018) – Timothy O'Conner and Christopher Franklin, "Free Will," Stanford Encyclopedia of Philosophy (Summer 2019 Edition), Edward N. Zalta (ed.), forthcoming, https://plato.stanford.edu/archives/sum2019/entries/freewill/.

Patterson and Thompson (2015) – Rubin Patterson and Giselle Thompson, "Transnational Factors Driving U.S. Inequality and Poverty" in Stephen Nathan Haymes, María Vidal de Haymes, and Reuben Jonathan Miller (eds.) The Routledge Handbook of Poverty in the United States (New York: Routledge, 2015) 33-42.

Penney (2019) – Darby Penney, "Child Homeless: A Growing Crisis," Substance Abuse and Mental Health Services Administration, original publication 2015, updated 2019, available at https://www.samhsa.gov/homelessness-programs-resources/hpr-resources/child-homelessness-growing-crisis.

Pereboom (1995) – Derk Pereboom, "Determinism Al Dente," Noûs, 29(1): 21–45. doi:10.2307/2215725

Pereboom (2001) – Derk Pereboom, Living Without Free Will, (Cambridge: Cambridge University Press, 2001).

Pereboom (2002a) – Derk Pereboom, "Living Without Free Will: The Case for Hard Incompatibilism", in Robert Kane (ed.), The Oxford Handbook of Free Will (New York: Oxford University Press, 2002), 477–488.

Pereboom (2002b) – Derk Pereboom, "Meaning in Life Without Free Will", Philosophical Exchange, 33: 18–34 (2002).

Pereboom (2007) – Derk Pereboom, "Hard Incompatibilism" in John Martin Fischer, Robert Kane, Derk Pereboom, and Manuel Vargas , Four Views on Free Will (Great Debates in Philosophy) (Malden, MA: Blackwell Publishing, 2007) 85-125.

Pereboom (2009) – Derk Pereboom, "Free Will, Love and Anger", Ideas y Valores, 58(141) (2009) 169–189.

Pereboom (2009-2) – Derk Pereboom (ed.), Free Will (Hackett Readings in Philosophy) (Cambridge, MA: Hackett Publishing Company, 2009).

Pereboom (2012) – Derk Pereboom, "Free Will Skepticism, Blame, and Obligation", in D. Justin Coates and Neal A. Tognazzini (eds.), Blame: Its Nature and Norms (New York: Oxford University Press, 2012) 189–206. doi:10.1093/acprof:oso/9780199860821.003.0010

Pereboom (2013) – Derk Pereboom, "Optimistic Skepticism About Free Will", in Paul Russell and Oisín Deery (eds.), The Philosophy of Free Will: Selected Contemporary Readings (New York: Oxford University Press, 2013) 421–49.

Bibliography

Pereboom (2014) – Derk Pereboom, Free Will, Agency, and Meaning in Life, Oxford: Oxford University Press, doi:10.1093/acprof:oso/9780199685516.001.0001

Posner (1996) – Richard A. Posner (ed.), The Essential Holmes (Chicago: The University of Chicago Press, 1996).

Rawls (1971) – John Rawls, A Theory of Justice, (Cambridge, MA: Harvard University Press, 1971)

Repetti (2017) – Riccardo Repetti, "What Do Buddhists Think About Free Will?" in Jake H. Davis and Owen Flanagan, A Mirror Is For Reflection: Understanding Buddhist Ethics (Oxford, UK: Oxford University Press, 2017).

Rickless (2016) – Samuel Rickless, "Locke On Freedom", *The Stanford Encyclopedia of Philosophy* (Winter 2016 Edition), Edward N. Zalta (ed.), https://plato.stanford.edu/archives/win2016/entries/locke-freedom/

Robinson (2017) – Howard Robinson, "Dualism", *The Stanford Encyclopedia of Philosophy* (Fall 2017 Edition), Edward N. Zalta (ed.), https://plato.stanford.edu/archives/fall2017/entries/dualism/

Saez and Zucman (2016) – Emmanuel Saez and Gabriel Zucman, Wealth Inequality in the United States Since 1913: Evidence From Capitalized Income Tax Data," Quarterly Journal of Economics, Vol. 131, Issue 2 (May 2016).

Salles (2005) – Ricardo Salles, The Stoics on Determinism and Compatibilism, (New York: Routledge, 2005).

Sapolsky (2016) – Robert Sapolsky, Behave: The Biology of Humans at Our Best and at Our Worst (New York: Penguin Press, 2017).

Satel and Lilienfeld (2013) – Sally Satel and Scott O. Lilienfeld, Brainwashed: The Seductive Appleal of Mindless Neuroscience, (New York: Basic Books, 2013).

Saunders (2017) – Tristram Fane Saunders, "Is Deckard a Replicant? The History of Blade Runner's Most Enduring Mystery," The Telegraph, Telegraph Media Group, 5 Oct. 2017, https://www.telegraph.co.uk/films/0/deckard-replicant-history-blade-runners-enduring-mystery.

Scanlon (1988) – T.M. Scanlon, "The Significance of Choice," in S.M. McMurrin (ed.), The Tanner Lectures on Human Values, (Salt Lake City: University of Utah Press, 1988) 149-217.

Scanlon (2008) – T.M. Scanlon, Moral Dimensions: Permissibility, Meaning, Blame (Cambridge MA: Harvard University Press, 2008).

Shakespeare (2003, orig. 1623) – Shakespeare, William. Macbeth, edited by Barbara Mowat and Paul Werstine, Simon & Schuster Publishing, Folger Shakespeare Library, 1st ed., 2003. Print.

Shariff et al. (2014) – A. F. Shariff, J. D. Greene, J. C. Karremans, J. B. Luguri, C. J. Clark, J. W. Schooler, R. F. Baumeister, K. D. Vohs, 'Free will and punishment: A mechanistic view of human nature reduces retribution', Psychological Science, published online 10 June 2014. pp. 1–8.

Speed, et. al. (2018) – David Speed, Thomas J. Coleman, III, and Joseph, "What Do You Mean, "What Does It All

Mean?": Atheism, Nonreligion, and Life Meaning," Sage Open, Volume 8, Issue 1 Available online at https://journals.sagepub.com/doi/10.1177/2158244017754238.

States (1987) – Bert O. States, "Hamlet's Older Brother," The Hudson Review, Vol. 39, No. 4 (Winter, 1987), pp. 537-552, (New York: The Hudson Review, Inc, 1987).

Shepherd (2017) – Joshua Shepherd, "Neuroscientific Threats to Free Will," published in Kevin Timpe, Meghan Griffith, and Neil Levy, The Routledge Companion to Free Will (New York: Routledge, 2017) 423-433. Available online at https://www.ncbi.nlm.nih.gov/books/NBK51 3665/pdf/Bookshelf_NBK513665.pdf.

Smilansky (2017) – Saul Smilansky, "Nonstandard Views," published in Kevin Timpe, Meghan Griffith, and Neil Levy, The Routledge Companion to Free Will (New York: Routledge, 2017) 136-146.

Spinoza (1670 [2001]) – Benedictus de Spinoza, Theological-Political Treatise, Samuel Shirley (Translator), Hackett Publishing Company, Inc., 2nd ed., 2001.

Spinoza (1677 [1985]) – Benedictus de Spinoza, Ethics, in Edwin Curley (ed. and tr.), The Collected Works of Spinoza, Vol. 1 (Princeton, NJ: Princeton University Press, 1985).

Spinoza (1677 [2014]) – Benedict de Spinoza, Ethics, Translated from the Latin by R. H. M. Elwes (South Australia: The University of Adelaide Library, web edition: ebooks@adelaide, 2014), https://ebooks.adelaide.edu.au /s/spinoza/benedict/ethics/index.html

Spinoza (1677 [2019]) – Benedict de Spinoza, The Ethics (Ethica Ordine Geometrico Demonstrata) Translated from the Latin by R. H. M. Elwes, http://www.sacred-texts.com/phi/spinoza/ethics/eth01.htm

Stent (2002) – Gunther S. Stent, "Paradoxes of Free Will," Transactions of the American Philosophical Society, (American Philosophical Society, 2002), New Series, Vol. 92, No. 6, 275-284, https://www.jstor.org/stable/4144913.

Strawson (1962) – Peter F. Strawson, "Freedom and Resentment", Proceedings of the British Academy, 48: 1–2, reprinted in Gary Watson (ed.), Free will (New York: Oxford University Press, 1982) 59–80.

Tax Policy Center (2016) – Tax Policy Center (The Urban Institute and Brookings Institution), "Median Value of Family Net Worth by Race or Ethnicity," 2016. Available at https://www.taxpolicycenter.org/fiscal-fact/median-value-wealth-race-ff03112019

Taylor (2010) – C.C.W. Taylor (ed.), The Atomists: Leucippus and Democritus: Fragments, reprint ed., 2010, University of Toronto Press.

Tolstoy (1869, translation 2007) – Leo Tolstoy, War and Peace, translated by Richard Pevear and Larissa Volokhonsky, Vintage Classics, 2007.

Turing (1950) – A. M. Turing, "Computing Machinery and Intelligence," Mind, New Series, Vol. 59, No. 236 (Oxford University Press 1950), pp. 433-460.

USDA (2018) – United States Department of Agriculture, "Food Security in the U.S.: Key Statistics and Graphics," available online at https://www.ers.usda.gov/topics/food-nutrition-assistance/food-security-in-the-us/key-statistics-graphics.aspx

Bibliography

USDA (2019) – United States Department of Agriculture, available at https://www.ers.usda.gov/topics/food-nutrition-assistance/food-security-in-the-us/key-statistics-graphics.aspx#:~:text=In%202019%3A,with%20adults%2C%20were%20food%20insecure.

Vargas (2007) – Manuel Vargas, "Revisionism" in John Martin Fischer, Robert Kane, Derk Pereboom, and Manuel Vargas, Four Views on Free Will (Great Debates in Philosophy) (Malden, MA: Blackwell Publishing, 2007) 126-165.

Vihvelin (2004) – Kadri Vihvelin, "Free Will Demystified: A Dispositional Account," Philosophical Topics, 32: 427–50.

Vohs and Schooler (2008) – K. D. Vohs and J. W. Schooler, The value of believing in free will encouraging a belief in determinism increases cheating. 19 *Psychol. Sci.* 49–54 (2008), available at https://assets.csom.umn.edu/assets/91974.pdf

Weinberg (1999) – Steven Weinberg, "A Designer Universe," New York Review of Books, October 21, 1999. Available online at https://www.nybooks.com/articles/1999/10/21/a-designer-universe/ and at https://www.physlink.com/Education/essay_weinberg.cfm.

Wetzel (2001) – James Wetzel, "Predestination, Pelagianism, and Foreknowledge," *The Cambridge Companion to Augustine,* Eleonore Stump & Norman Kretzmann (eds.), Cambrdige University Press, pp. 49-58.

Wolff (2017) – Edward N. Wolff, "Household Wealth Trends in the United States, 1962 to 2016: Has Middle Class Wealth Recovered?" National Bureau of Economic

AFREEISM

Research, Working Paper 24085 (November 2017). Available at https://www.nber.org/papers/w24085.pdf.

www.ingramcontent.com/pod-product-compliance
Lightning Source LLC
Chambersburg PA
CBHW030239030426
42336CB00009B/165